Assassinations that Shaped
the Twentieth Century

Assassinations that Shaped the Twentieth Century

Phil Carradice

First published in Great Britain in 2025 by
Pen & Sword History
An imprint of Pen & Sword Books Limited
Yorkshire – Philadelphia

ISBN 978 1 39905 379 2

Typeset by Mac Style
Printed in the UK by CPI Group (UK) Ltd, Croydon, CR0 4YY.

The Publisher's authorised representative in the EU for product
safety is Authorised Rep Compliance Ltd., Ground Floor,
71 Lower Baggot Street, Dublin D02 P593, Ireland.
www.arccompliance.com

For a complete list of Pen & Sword titles please contact

PEN & SWORD BOOKS LIMITED
47 Church Street, Barnsley, South Yorkshire, S70 2AS, England
E-mail: enquiries@pen-and-sword.co.uk
Website: www.pen-and-sword.co.uk
or
PEN AND SWORD BOOKS
1950 Lawrence Road, Havertown, PA 19083, USA
E-mail: uspen-and-sword@casematepublishers.com
Website: www.penandswordbooks.com

Dedication

This book is dedicated to the memory of my father, John Matheson Carradice, who spent hours with me discussing assassinations, political and private, as works of history. In his memory, Trudy and I wandered through New Delhi and Amritsar, stood at the site of Gandhi's assassination, marvelled at the Golden Temple and knew what he meant when he declared: 'You've got to go there to appreciate it – whatever the *it* may be.' Thanks Dad.

And, as ever, to my darling Trudy. Without you, sweetheart, nothing I have ever written would have been possible. Treasured memories. One day we will be together again.

Acknowledgements

Kath Giblin of Bardic Books
The members of Llantwit Major Writers Group

Contents

Chapter One

Assassination in the Modern World

Since the beginning of recorded history, the use of assassination as a political tool has been a devastatingly constant practice. Men, women and children have all been 'put to the sword' for a wide range of reasons and purposes. Their deaths have not always been effective, but you can be sure that each decade brings with it a whole series of assassination attempts.

The ancient world was awash with political killings. From the death of Pharaoh Teti, the first recorded victim of political murder, to Emperor Charlemagne's killing of over 4,000 Germanic tribesmen in just one day during the Dark Ages, assassination was a wild and often flamboyant means of destroying enemies. And it did not stop with Charlemagne's Germanic massacre in 782 CE.

The death of 4,000 enemy tribesmen may mark a temporary zenith, the end of an epoch, but it was never the end of the process. Assassination went on and on throughout the centuries. It proliferated in the Middle Ages, in the Reformation years and in the days that followed, up to and including the present day.

Then and now, assassination was always a far cheaper method of defeating opponents than waging a formal and traditional war, in both monetary expenditure and the numbers of casualties sustained. It might not have been as glamorous or frightening as serried ranks of uniformed warriors suddenly appearing over the hilltop, but it has certainly been effective.

Assassination has not always worked, but at times, and for a variety of reasons, it has been far more efficient than gathering together vast armies, perhaps 40,000 or 50,000 strong, and hurling them at each other's throats. As a result, over the centuries, the act of assassination has grown into something more than mere happenstance. It has become an accepted political and military enterprise, one which even now remains in use.

That assessment, of course, totally ignores the by-product, the unexpected and unlooked-for results of assassination. The 1942 murder plot against Reinhard Heydrich in Czechoslovakia, for example, was a hugely successful enterprise, an action that removed one of the most malevolent and evil members of the Nazi Party. Yet in other ways it was a total and terrible failure, causing the deaths of 1,300 innocent men, women and children, killed in a horrendous example of reprisals in the Czech villages of Lidice and Lezaky. That was something for which nobody had planned or expected.

However you look at it, the deliberate and premeditated killing of an opponent can never be declared a civilized tactic. But wherever and whenever it is used, assassination has been employed to achieve a wide range of ambitions and values. The results, perhaps inevitably, have been what might be expected – never acceptable, but sometimes effective. It depends largely on how you view the act of assassination:

'Assassination is an act of war and must be approached as such …
[It is] a David and Goliath contest where cunning and surprise overcome brute force.'[1]

The victims of assassination invariably achieve a degree of fame and notoriety they might otherwise never have attained. The assassins, on the other hand, are usually relegated to the background of history. Brutus, Cassius and the other assassins of Julius Caesar are largely remembered because of Shakespeare's play, not their actions.

There are many more notable examples. Think of the assassination of Archbishop Thomas Becket in 1170. Can anyone remember the names of the killers who answered King Henry II's plea for someone to rid him of his 'turbulent priest'? Nine times out of ten, the answer will be 'No'. For the killers, it was a case of job done, followed by a retreat to a well-deserved life of insignificance and ignominy.

Assassination as a tool, as a piece of political machinery, has always remained an option for ambitious men. In the ancient world, it was rife, the Egyptians and the Romans making it virtually a social and religious imperative when plots and plans began to go wrong.

And yet, regardless of a proliferation of assassinations in the ancient world, it is the twentieth century, with all its social, educational, military and political benefits, that has to go on record as being one of the most brutal periods of assassination in the whole course of history.

In a single century, thousands have fallen before the bullets, bombs and knife blades of assassins. In Germany alone, in the four years between 1918 and 1922, more than 350 men and women were killed. That was during the early days of the Weimar Republic, when German culture and politics were in a state of unrest following the country's defeat in the First World War.

It was followed, of course, by the advent of Hitler's Nazi Party, when assassination through events such as The Night of the Long Knives, Kristallnacht and the Holocaust became an expected part of government routine. Very few of the 10 million victims of the Holocaust were ever publicly named, but they were all victims of assassination. Russia was not far behind the Germans in compiling a terrifyingly long list of victims.

Intolerance and a self-indulgent belief in the misplaced theory that 'my way is the right and only way' has led to a wide degree of intolerance and blood-letting. The twentieth century was an age which, despite witnessing the greatest technological advances ever recorded, can only ever be regarded as a hundred years of brutality.

That, leads to the obvious question – does assassination ever actually work? It is a generalized question that can only lead to a pack of generalized answers. Even so, they are worth looking at.

All too often, the death of one tyrant or dictator has simply produced another man or woman of the same character. The aims of the assassins – admirable or acceptable as they might possibly have been – somehow seem to get lost in the whirlwind of chaos and confusion which has just destroyed the status quo. That leads, inevitably, to the unanswerable but still attractive dilemma of 'What if?'.

If the July Bomb Plot of 1944 had gone the other way and if Claus von Stauffenberg's bomb had managed to eliminate Adolf Hitler, would it have brought an earlier and less costly end to the death camps and the barbaric final few months of the Second World War? Or would it have provoked a furore from the military and the citizens of the 'motherland', as Hitler insisted on calling Germany?

Would Mahatma Gandhi, had he not fallen before an assassin's bullets in 1948, have succeeded in uniting the Muslims and the Hindus of a newly independent India? Or would his admittedly puzzling greatness have led to more riots and murder? Such questions are imponderable, with no easy answers. Perhaps that is what makes the issue of assassination so interesting for the reader and historian.

After the assassination of Abraham Lincoln in 1865, British Prime Minister Benjamin Disraeli stood up in Parliament and declared: 'Assassination has never changed the history of the world.'[2]

Disraeli's statement has not stopped assassination happening again and again, and someone as astute as he would have known that the murder of politicians, war leaders, dignitaries and even sportsmen would continue long after he had left this earth.

Arguably, assassination merely inflames the temper and passions of those who are left floundering in the wake of a public killing. The knee-jerk reaction has never been as strong as it is in the minds and bodies of comrades and friends after an assassination. The long-term effects can be equally damaging, probably even more so.

We are left with hope that the terrorism exhibited during the twentieth century – because terrorism is what modern-day assassination really is – will come to an end, and sooner rather than later.

* * *

Looking back on it now, the twentieth century seems to have been filled with example after example of political assassinations, their regularity and significance rivalling in notoriety even major catastrophes like the two world wars.

In part, this was because the end of those wars facilitated the breakup of longstanding empires, which went on to help create new states, new countries, new empires even. Old regimes may have needed changing or even destruction, but they had at least been familiar.

As in the establishment of most new entities, the political and territorial changes post-1918 and 1945 brought dissatisfaction and dispute before the leaders, politicians and even the citizens of the new nations were able to create an equilibrium that pleased everyone.

Ernst Rohm, leader of Hitler's private army of thugs and bully boys known as the SA (Sturmabteilung), once declared that revolution should never be a one-off event, but must inevitably be followed by a second, maybe even a third rebellion. He was clear that kicking at the foundations of any new creation, however beautiful those foundations might seem, was essential if the results of the revolution were to last.

Such a belief, of course, was self-destructive and spelled the end of Rohm. The subsequent culling of his SA in what became known as The Night of the Long Knives provided what was, effectively, Nazi Germany's second revolution.

However, it is only fair to say that in the twentieth century, particularly during its second half, things have gone beyond the concept of a 'second revolution', beyond the confusion inherent in the creation of new states. In particular, that is certainly the case in the years after 1945:

'The period since the Second World War has been dominated by states using assassinations to remove dissidents and investigative journalists representing a threat to their power.'[3]

The above quotation is true enough, but it does not tell the whole story. The efforts of terrorist groups like the IRA and Sri Lanka's

Tamil Tigers are only the tip of the iceberg. Since 1945, politicians, statesmen and military leaders have, on a regular basis, been targets – or would-be targets – for assassination, but so too have people such as film stars, singers, poets and artists.

You cannot imagine people like Chopin, John Constable or George Formby being likely victims of assassination. But what of John Lennon, Ross McWhirter, Andy Warhol, Salman Rushdie and even John Wayne? At one time or another, they were all potential or actual assassination targets. There were many others.

The reasons for the sudden elevation of popular media figures into the sights of assassins' guns or within range of their bombs are many and varied. Breaking down those reasons, you soon discover that they include a media policy of greatly increased exposure for the so-called 'stars'.

It is a degree of exposure that has obsessed the wounded minds of many members of society who, until the coming of increased media coverage, were regarded as criminals. They were never acknowledged or allowed to be recognized as being ill and in need of emotional help.

Public acknowledgement of the victim's wealth and fame, along with a desire on the part of the assassin to claim some of that fame for him or herself, have also played a part. It is jealousy on an immense scale, something rarely seen before.

Perhaps more than anything else, the growth of 'celebrity-chasing' has brought with it significant vulnerability for pop stars and the like.

Mental health issues are not new, but the attitude of modern media, along with supposed benefits such as easy access to travel across the world and disposable monetary assets, have contributed towards increased pressure on fragile personalities, making public figures more vulnerable than they have ever been.

Nowhere, it seems, is anyone safe. After the death of John Lennon, his old comrade George Harrison grew so paranoid about safety that he covered the grounds around his home outside London with cameras, electric warning devices and alarms of all sorts.

Harrison had placed so many devices around his house that the locals took to calling the place Fort Knox. Nevertheless, it did not stop

Michael Abram breaking in, stabbing Harrison forty times, puncturing his lung and being a few millimetres away from killing him.[4]

* * *

It is logical to assume that assassins – ancient and modern alike – believed in the validity of what they were doing. Assassinations, unlike the riots and reactive lashings and thrashings that symbolize murder or mob violence, are usually planned, the killers knowing exactly the purpose of their actions and their expected result.

It is invariably the general public, the man and woman in the street, who are taken by surprise. Once again, it is a disruption of the status quo, a disruption which, until the blaring headlines smashed them in their faces, had meant very little to them.

Some of the assassins, particularly those employed as and by government agents, who desire nothing more than the destruction of potential opponents, operate in groups. These multi-assassin murders have shocked not just those close to the victim but the whole world.

Take the assassination of Egyptian Prime Minister Anwar el-Sadat in 1981. The killing was carried out by a large number of Muslim fundamentalists; two were killed on the spot and twenty-four were indicted for murder and conspiracy, five of them eventually being executed for the crime. The others were sentenced to long periods in jail. The shock and outrage at the killing of a man who had, just a few years before, along with Israeli PM Menachem Begin, been awarded the Nobel Prize for Peace, was exactly what the assassins were looking for. The enormity of the killing, with Sadat hit by at least forty bullets, ensured its notoriety and finality.[5]

Other assassins during the twentieth century were solo artists who operated out of motives ranging from grudges against the victims to their own serious mental health problems. Arguably, the solo assassin, the lone wolf, has always been hardest to identify, the most difficult to eliminate or capture.

At the same time, the motives of these isolated killers do seem to be more personal than those who act in unison or partnership with others:

'Arthur Bremer, who shot and wounded George Wallace, has lamented his failure to achieve "Lee Harvey Oswald type" assassin's fame … Ronald Reagan's [would-be] assassin wanted to impress an actress … Rebecca Schaeffer's assassin [another actress] was in love with her.'[6]

Investigative journalists are, by the nature of their profession, a particularly vulnerable group. They are men and women who have always been a specific and a potentially open target. Their work means that they are regularly victimized, perhaps more so now than at any other stage in history:

'Reporting the truth has become a dangerous business and the number of fatalities amongst journalists, both in war zones and in corrupt countries, grows steadily … Attempts to uncover seediness and criminality in the age of the internet and global communications have become extremely costly.'[7]

From people like Daphne Caruana Galizia of Malta, who was killed by a car bomb in 2017, to cameraman Samer Abu Daqqa, who perished in an Israeli air strike in 2023, the death toll of journalists continues to rise. It shows no sign of ever going away.

Welshman Gareth Jones, the reporter who first exposed Stalin's deliberately contrived famine in Ukraine in the 1930s – a holocaust by any other name – was one of the most notable victims. Stalin's response to the tragedy in Ukraine was the cold-blooded murder of several million people, and in 1935, Jones, by then in Japanese-occupied Mongolia, was kidnapped and shot by local forces. Was it assassination? The jury is still out.

*   *   *

From 1900 onwards, the assassination of major world figures became, if not commonplace, at least something that happened on a fairly regular basis. The advent of effective and easy-to-use firearms meant that almost anyone who had the money to buy a revolver was now in a position of great power.

In the fourteen years leading up to the outbreak of the First World War in 1914, the killing of kings, presidents and, bizarre as it might first appear, even the demise of cowboy heroes like Pat Garrett dominated the press. They perished along with many other minor figures who, by dying before their time, ensured themselves a degree of brief fame.

The period culminated, of course, with the assassination of the Archduke Franz Ferdinand, heir to the throne of Austria-Hungary, and of his wife, Sophie.

In a blisteringly hot summer, 1914 was a time when the main concern of the British newspapers was not the assassination of some obscure Austrian nobleman but the cricket scores and the racing results.

The deaths of Franz Ferdinand and Sophie warranted initial headlines, then declined to a series of brief columns in the newspapers of the time. Even Kaiser Wilhelm, the belligerent German Emperor, was slow to take advantage of the situation. That soon began to change.

Within six weeks, the consequences of the assassinations of Franz Ferdinand and Sophie had snowballed in significance. The ramifications of that one act of violence were enormous, and by the end of the broiling summer of 1914, virtually the whole of the Western world was at war. Other nations soon joined in the conflict, making this the first world-wide war in the history of humankind.

The death of Franz Ferdinand was perhaps the most monumental assassination since the killing of Julius Caesar. The effects of Gavrilo Princip's two shots echoed, almost literally, around the world. More of the archduke, his wife and his killer later.

Chapter Two

The Lead Up to War, 1900–1914

In 1900, nobody would have dreamed that a world-wide war was about to erupt. The thought of well over 10 million casualties – civilian and military – was beyond the imagination of most people. Localised wars were common enough; they could be coped with relatively easily. Global conflict was something different, but was arguably something that could have been stifled at birth.

Politicians and statesmen of the 'big' nations should have known what was lurking in the shadows. Perhaps they did, but they certainly chose not to delve too deeply. If people had cared to look for them, however, the hints were there. Change was in the air.

The year 1900 was not, in itself, one of specific developments or new directions. But enough happened to give an inkling of what was coming to all those who cared or wondered what the new century might bring. Not just the start of a new era, 1900 was a precursor to major changes that were about to hit the world.

The Boer War was beginning to rumble to a close, with victories and defeats on both sides – a considerable change from the early days of the conflict, when everything seemed to be going in favour of the Boers. Pretoria, the Boer capital, now fell to the British, while Mafeking and Kimberley were soon relieved, but, as if to even the score, the second Battle of Spion Kop resulted in a definite victory for the Boers. However, Lord Kitchener was now in charge of British forces in South Africa, a factor that, more than anything else, spelled a different kind of war to come.

Meanwhile, the Olympic Games were held in France, the Commonwealth of Australia was proclaimed, the first modern submarine was launched and Graf Von Zeppelin's ominous lighter-than-air dirigibles first flew in the skies above Germany. Queen Victoria, then Britain's longest-reigning monarch, was clearly approaching the end of her life – that would come the following year.

In particular, there were two events which showed clearly and dangerously the way the world was going. In April 1900, there was an unsuccessful attempt to kill the Prince of Wales, the failed assassin claiming he was striking a blow for the Boer Republic. Then, just two months later, came the successful assassination of King Umberto of Italy.

Umberto I, King of Italy, Milan (assassinated 1900)

Umberto Rainerio had become King of Italy in January 1878. He ascended to the throne just fifteen years after the third and final Italian War of Independence, when the various independent and conquered states of the country became free of external ownership and were united under one ruler. The country took the name of Italy and appointed Umberto's father, Victor Emmanuel II, as king.

When, after due time, Umberto became king he was not inclined towards leniency. He had led a torrid, not to say toxic, childhood, his father disliking and not trusting him. He had to stand to attention whenever Emmanuel entered the room and, in public and in private, before talking to him, Umberto had to kneel and kiss his hand. Love and affection were clearly lacking in his life. Poorly educated, Umberto never read books and had little regard either for culture or academe.

Umberto's reign saw the realigned Italian nation expand its influence into the Horn of Africa and move on to form the Triple Alliance with Germany and Austria-Hungary. A strong militarist, Umberto had seen action in various Italian Wars of Independence, commanding the Royal Sardinian Army with some skill. Unfortunately for him, his reign coincided with social unrest and economic problems across most of Europe. He responded with something of a crackdown on socialism within Italy.

As a result of Umberto's anti-socialist views, he became hated by the left-wing workers of the country. The 1898 Bava Beccaris Massacre in Milan, when more than eighty demonstrators against food shortages were shot down by the military, merely increased Umberto's unpopularity with the socialists of his newly formed country.

There had been an unsuccessful attempt on his life in November 1878, just a few months after his accession to the throne. Umberto managed to ward off the blow and avoid the knife thrust, but the prime minister, who was walking with him at the time, was wounded. A further attempt on his life was made in April 1897, an out-of-work ironsmith trying to stab him.

Then in 1900 Umberto was killed by Gaetano Bresci, an Italian-American anarchist who had come to Italy with the deliberate intention of assassinating the king. He apparently brought his pistol with him from the USA, honing his shooting by taking hours of practice before making the attempt.

On the evening of 29 July 1900, Umberto was shot three times by Bresci, who claimed that he was a man of principle and was seeking revenge on the man he blamed for the Bava Beccaris Massacre and called 'the murderer king':

> 'I have not shot Umberto. I have killed a king. I have killed a principle.'[1]

The king had been on holiday near Milan, but on the afternoon of 29 July he took time to present medals at an athletics meeting. Climbing back into the state carriage as the meeting broke up, he was approached by Bresci, who fired into his body from close range. Three shots hit his chest and Umberto died instantly. The assassin was sentenced to life imprisonment on the island of Santo Stefano, but three years later was found dead in what were reported as 'mysterious circumstances'.

The assassination of King Umberto of Italy had significant repercussions around the world. Governing bodies in the USA became paranoid about political killings, an emotion that was added to by the violent death of President McKinley a year later. The 'land of the free' suddenly became a lot more difficult to enter.

There was another, much closer repercussion. It had been a long time since Abraham Lincoln had been assassinated, and Gaetano Bresci's action in killing King Umberto had set a precedent. Assassination was once more on the agenda of security men and would-be assassins. It had been the King of Italy today; who would it be tomorrow?

In 1906, the US Naturalization Act laid down the rule that all immigrants must swear to be patriotic to the USA – and only the USA. Bresci, as an immigrant to the USA, had clearly not abandoned deep and intense love of his old country.

President William McKinley, Buffalo, USA (assassinated 1901)

President McKinley was just six months into his second term as President of the USA when he was shot on 6 September 1901. He died from gangrene caused by the bullet eight days later, on 14 September.

McKinley was always a man of the people, happy to mingle with the crowds and shake their hands. It made him very popular, but his staff were not so happy; when McKinley indicated that he wished to go to the Pan-American Exposition in Buffalo, they twice cancelled the visit. McKinley put it back on the schedule for a third time. When advised that this, too, should be cancelled, the president refused to call off the visit yet again, convinced that no-one would want to hurt him.[2]

Like the killer of Italy's King Umberto, the assassin was another anarchist, an American by the name of Leon Czolgosz. He had recently lost his job and felt that McKinley, who had won a second term as US President on the ticket of improved economic conditions and regular jobs for the people, was to blame. McKinley had failed to provide either, Czolgosz felt – wrongly as it happened – and he decided that he had no other option but to kill the president.

Leon Czolgosz was the son of Polish immigrants. Born in Detroit in 1873, Czolgosz was a determined young man. He had made contact with several anarchist groups and individuals, in particular the noted and nationally recognized Emma Goldman, using the story that he was simply trying to find out more about the anarchist cause. Using the alias Frederick Nieman, he did not tell Goldman and other anarchists what his plan really was.

On 6 September, Czolgosz was part of the jostling crowd that was pushing forward to shake the president's hand as he returned to the Expo showground after a visit to a local landmark. The presidential party had been visiting places such as Niagara Falls each day, and now arrived back at the Expo on the presidential train. It was estimated that there were somewhere in the region of 115,000 spectators waiting to greet him. It was just after 4.00 pm.

What transpired were an eventful, not to say wild, few moments in time. The crowd screamed with excitement as the cannonade, fired to welcome the president back from his trip, roared out. Unfortunately, the cannons were located too close to the train and several carriage windows were shattered by the blast. Apparently, the only one not alarmed was President McKinley.

On his first attempt, the density of the crowd kept Czolgosz at a distance; despite pushing and shoving with all of his might, he could not get close. He tried again as McKinley was leaving the exhibition, this time coming face-to-face with his target. The president put out his hand to shake Czolgosz's right palm, exactly where the assassin was carrying the gun, concealed under a cloth. Czolgosz fired twice, the first bullet grazing the president but the second one lodging in his abdomen.

The general rule had been that the president would never shake a covered hand, but, coming face-to-face with Czolgosz, McKinley thought he was suffering from an injury and reached for the assassin's hidden gun hand. He had just given his 'lucky' red carnation flower to a young girl who had admired it. In both actions, McKinley placed himself in positions of grave danger – one from superstition, the other from an assassin's bullets.

As the bullets struck him, President McKinley lurched forward and Czolgosz stepped back, preparing to fire again. He stumbled heavily into the man standing behind him, an Afro-Caribbean native by the name of James Parker. Realizing what had happened, Parker grabbed at the gun and began wrestling with Czolgosz. Soldiers and bodyguards joined in, using their rifle butts to smash the assassin to the ground.

McKinley shouted out, ordering the beating to stop. His wound, he declared, was not serious. With Czolgosz now pulled to his feet and firmly restrained, one of the security men measured the distance and dropped the killer with a single blow.

McKinley, en route to hospital, suddenly jerked erect. Feeling in the lining of his coat, he had grasped the assassin's first bullet, which had apparently been deflected by a metal button. The other bullet was never found. There was no exit wound, the bullet presumably remaining in his body, and the injury was clearly significant.

The doctors at the hospital were inexperienced and the facilities limited. A piece of cloth was found in the wound, and this was removed. McKinley was then taken to Milburn House, where he was staying. He was met his distraught wife, a rather nervous women who had left the presidential party some hours before.

Over the next few days, McKinley appeared to be recovering. As the danger apparently passed, Vice-President Theodore 'Teddy' Roosevelt felt able to leave Milburn House and embark on a delayed vacation. Several other dignitaries did the same.

Then, early on13 September, McKinley collapsed. He lapsed into and out of consciousness throughout the day, clearly knowing that he was dying. 'It is useless, gentlemen,' he told his doctors and servants. He died at 2.15 am on 14 September 1901.[3]

McKinley was a large man, possibly even obese, and modern thinking now declares that his size delayed the advance of gangrene in his body.

If the bullet could have been found and removed, if medical diagnosis and treatment had been better, the president might have survived.

In the wake of McKinley's death, there was an immediate backlash. Quite apart from the passing of the US Naturalization Act within a few years, public opinion swung violently against the various anarchist groups then operating in the USA. Emma Goldman, anarchist and friend of Leon Czolgosz, was arrested and detained in prison for three weeks. She was finally released without any charges being levelled against her.

The houses and offices of various anarchists were attacked and damaged, with anarchist newspapers closed down. Individual anarchists – or suspected anarchists – were abused in the street. The popularity of President McKinley guaranteed some sort of response – and it was all so unnecessary.

Some days before the assassination, Leon Czolgosz was seen in the street carrying two revolvers, one of them the identical weapon used to kill Italian monarch Umberto just the year before. The sighting was referred to the police who were handling the president's security, but nothing was done. From that point on, all security of US Presidents was passed to the Secret Service.

Czolgosz was immediately sent for trial. Found guilty, he was condemned to death in the electric chair. He was duly executed on 25 October 1901.

Emile Zola, Writer, Paris (assassinated 1902)

It was not just kings and presidents who met their end at the hands of assassins during the early days of the twentieth century. The French writer, playwright and journalist Emile Zola was assassinated in September 1902.

A major figure in the liberalization of French culture, Zola was one of several artists to take up the cause of Alfred Dreyfus. His newspaper article on the Dreyfus Affair, headlined under the aggressive title of

'*J'accuse*', held nothing back. Dreyfus was a Jewish army officer who, Zola proclaimed, was a victim of rampant anti-Semitism. Zola wrote that he was being victimized by the authorities, wrongly accused of passing military secrets to the Germans.

Arrested in 1894 and sentenced to prison on Devil's Island, Dreyfus and his case attracted huge media attention across the world. Even after the 'guilty' verdict, Zola and others kept fighting for the release of Dreyfus, something that infuriated right-wing groups in French politics.

Zola's denouncement of the authorities, the military and anyone opposed to Dreyfus was so virulent that he was accused of criminal libel, and in February 1898 he was forced to flee to England, where he spent six unhappy months. Accused of morbid hypochondria, he nearly destroyed his marriage to Alexandrine Meley by conducting an open affair with Jeanne Rozerot, with whom he had a number of children.

Highly critical of the President of the French Second Republic, Zola's lifestyle trod an uneasy line between a comfortable existence and a dangerous precipice that could lead only to disaster. He died on 29 September 1902, the victim of deliberate carbon monoxide poisoning.

A chimney sweep/roofer who was repairing the chimney of the house next-door later claimed that he had deliberately blocked the chimney to Zola's apartment. His motive, however, remained unclear. Whatever that motive might have been, the result of the simple action on the roof of the apartment buildings was the poisoning that killed the great writer.

Zola and Alexandrine had been away, and on their return lit the fire in their bedroom to take the chill out of the house. Windows and doors were closed, and soon noxious fumes were swirling around the bedroom. Zola and Alexandrine woke at 3.00 am, feeling sick, but Zola refused to allow his wife to call the servants. It was, he thought, a simple case of indigestion. When he did finally get out of bed, he fell unconscious to the floor.

Servants, alarmed by the non-appearance of Zola and his wife, went into the bedroom at 9.00 am, and doctors were immediately called. They worked on Zola for twenty minutes, but it was too late – he was dead. Alexandrine was taken to a nearby clinic, where she soon recovered.

Fifty thousand people turned up for Zola's funeral, including Alfred Dreyfus, who had finally been declared innocent and released.

The French authorities carried out tests on the anthracite coal that had been used and on other batches just like it, but could find no trace of carbon monoxide. It was almost half a century later, in 1953, before the rooftop workman's involvement was revealed in an article in a French newspaper, the strange death of Emile Zola having remained unexplained until then.[4]

Russia's Bloody Sunday, St Petersburg, Russia (9 January 1905)

The events and results of Russia's 1917 Revolution are known by most people. They are there, in front of you, whenever you open a newspaper or turn on the television set, with news of the latest events involving Russia. Good or bad, helpless, hopeless or indifferent, you cannot ignore the power and the effect of that 1917 Revolution.

There was, however, an earlier uprising in 1905, one that is not nearly so well known. This rising was distantly connected with the disastrous Russian war with Japan, a conflict that was still raging in the Far East. Defeats, at sea and on land, had destroyed Russian morale and standing in the world. The war marked the birth of a new empire, that of Japan, at the expense and possible demise of Russia.

In 1905, working-class unrest manifested itself in complaints about the living conditions of many thousands of Russian workers in the factories and small businesses of the cities. The main issues were dreadful working conditions, the length of the working day, poor wages, lack of good housing and poor food supplies. Together, they led to one of the most brutal and bloodthirsty mass assassinations in Russian history – known as the Bloody Sunday Massacre.

On the morning of Sunday, 9 January 1905, an unarmed, peaceful demonstration and protest march, led by the popular preacher Father

Gregory Gapon, headed for the czar's Winter Palace in St Petersburg. None of the marchers had any intention of spreading violence. They viewed the czar as the soul of their country, 'The Little Father', as he was called. He was not just an omnipotent ruler; he was a man who would, when he realized the seriousness of their position, aid them in their struggle just to survive.

The intention of the marchers was to present Czar Nicholas II with a petition, a document that highlighted the position of the workers in Russian society. That position was easily identified. They and their families were at the bottom of everything – with no political representation, slum housing and overlong working days, they had nothing that could help them to ease a life of strain and poverty.

The emancipation of the serfs in 1861 had been a welcome development, but it had also caused a significant social problem for Russian society. Previously, serfs had been restricted to working on the land, toiling for the great Russian aristocrats. Emancipation created a new peasant working class, no longer confined to the land but without the infrastructure to support their existence and gradual move away from the countryside into the urban jungle of the towns and cities.

The rigid discipline required for working in the factories, along with an almost total lack of safety precautions, began as an irritation and soon developed into a festering sore. Political and socialist groups such as the Bolsheviks and the Mensheviks muddied the water on one side, while the Okhrana and other government factions did the same at the opposite extreme. It was a situation that would eventually mould itself into a recipe for total disaster.

The Bloody Sunday marchers came from various parts of the city, joining up in the early afternoon. Waiting to greet them, posted at various positions around the Winter Palace and in the surrounding streets, were somewhere in the region of 10,000 infantry from the czar's Imperial Guard. Cavalry units, mostly regular troops and Cossacks, added to the strength of the palace defenders. Opinions vary about the number of protesters; the claim that there were 50,000 of them seemingly a gross exaggeration. A figure of around 3,000 would be a good estimate.

The order to open fire on the marchers was given by one of the officers of the Imperial Guard, a fairly low level for such momentous decision-making. The absence of Czar Nicholas from the Winter Palace, a fact unknown to the marchers, and the heavy conglomeration of soldiers around it would seem to indicate that this was no accidental event, rather, a carefully planned and executed example of mass assassination.

The individual who fired the first shot remains unknown, but around 2.00 pm it came, like a bolt from the blue. It was not just the marchers who came under fire. Unsuspecting and innocent family groups out for a Sunday walk along the Nevsky Prospect in the rear of the marchers were also targets for a defence force that was soon out of control.

The opening salvo was accompanied by a cavalry charge from the Cossacks and the regular cavalry, men, women and children being trampled underfoot:

> 'Cossacks galloped rapidly towards us with drawn swords. So, then, it was to be a massacre after all. Our front ranks broke before them, opening to right and left, and down this lane the soldiers drove their horses, striking on both sides.'[5]

Quite why the order to fire was given remains clouded in mystery. The marchers were singing hymns and patriotic dirges, 'God Save the Czar' and so on. Father Gabon had notified the authorities of the march and its purpose, so there could be no claim that the demonstration was too big or that the marchers were out of control. But whatever the reason, volley after volley was poured into the crowd.

The czar and the royal family had left St Petersburg the night before, heading for the luxury of their palace at Tsarskoye Selo. They were not exactly running for cover, but the hope of government officials was that the police and the Okhrana, the state secret police, would spread the news of their departure. The march and the handing over of the petition would, it was believed, have to be rescheduled. However, this never happened.

It later transpired that there had been clashes between workers and soldiers across St Petersburg during the morning of 9 January. They were nothing compared to the shootings outside the Winter Palace, but it was clear that somebody, somewhere, was pulling strings in order to create a disaster.

Approximately forty protesters were killed in the opening minutes of the mass assassination, Father Gapon managing to slip away in the chaos, but the total number of deaths on Bloody Sunday is unclear. Czar Nicholas claimed there were ninety dead, along with 333 wounded and injured – nice round figures. Leon Trotsky was later to claim that many hundreds had died and that the czarist government had ordered the bodies to be secretly buried.

Adding in the passers-by who were caught up in the affair, a total of approximately 1,000 dead and injured would seem to be an accurate casualty figure. Czar Nicholas expressed his regret, claiming that the massacre was 'painful and sad'. The surviving marchers had a rather different take on the massacre – 'We no longer have a Czar,' they claimed.

The consequences of Bloody Sunday were vast. Public outrage, both in Russia and abroad, was enormous, international condemnation sweeping across Russia and all things Russian in a wave of monumental proportions. The old image of the Russian bear rose again, the vast and distant country once more dubbed as a land overflowing with ignorant peasants, uncivilized and uncaring.

Within, Russia the workers seemed to suddenly find a platform. Strikes, although technically illegal, erupted in St Petersburg and quickly spread to all of the industrial cities of the country. Prompted and unashamedly used by revolutionary parties, strikes and workers' actions continued for several years in what really was the start of the 1917 Revolution.

Czar Nicholas tried to appease the workers, calling a duma (parliament), but it was a toothless machine that satisfied nobody. It was eventually sheer violence and brutality that ended the chaos caused by Bloody Sunday.

Between October 1905 and April 1906, it is estimated that 15,000 peasants and workers were killed or executed, 20,000 injured and 45,000 sentenced to internal exile in Siberia. The czar, previously champion of the people, became no different from the rest of the Russian aristocracy and was held personally responsible for much of the unrest in the country.[6]

Pat Garrett, Texas (assassinated 29 February 1908)

The name Pat Garrett is synonymous with the death of American outlaw Billy the Kid. Real name Henry McCarthy or William Henry Bonney Jnr, depending on your reading of the evidence, Billy the Kid was tracked down and assassinated by Garrett in 1881.

It was a cold-blooded, deliberate assassination in the middle of the night, but it lies twenty years outside the scope of this book. Garrett's own death came twenty-seven years later in 1908, which fits perfectly into our timescale.

A relatively minor figure in terms of world history, Pat Garrett's significance lies not in his life, fascinating as that might be, but in his death. Like the presumed end of the train robbers Butch Cassidy and the Sundance Kid, Garrett's death was far more significant than anything else he set out to do in his life, including the killing of Billy the Kid.

The final years of all three – Cassidy and Sundance a little dubiously, as no-one really knows what happened to them in South America – marked the end of what we know as the Wild West. As the twentieth century unravelled, the emergence of a different world spelled the end of range riders and cattle drives, of Native American wars and the lonesome gun-hawk riding off into the sunset.

New technology brought instant communication between the east and west coasts of the USA. Cars, vans and other mechanical modes of transport replaced horses and stagecoaches, the law of the gun was gradually eclipsed and America began to develop its desire for empire. Garrett, like the outlaws Butch and Sundance, would probably not have been best pleased to see the changes.

Born in 1859, of English ancestry, Pat Garrett spent his early years on a plantation in Louisiana. The American Civil War destroyed the family finances, however, and Garrett moved west to make a living. At various times he was a buffalo hunter, a gunfighter and a cowboy on the big ranches of Texas. It was as a town sheriff and US Marshal that he made his name, working predominantly in Texas and New Mexico.

After writing a book, *The Authentic Life of Billy the Kid*, Garrett ran unsuccessfully for the Senate, spent one month as a Texas Ranger and then became Collector of Taxes for President Teddy Rosevelt. Together with Bat Masterson and Ben Daniels, he was renowned as one of the White House Gunfighters.

He was finally dismissed for incompetence in 1906 and, in deep financial difficulties, headed west again, this time to El Paso in Texas. He became a rancher but fell out with fellow cattleman Jesse Wayne Brazel over grazing rights. A meeting was arranged, Garrett and a friend called Carl Adamson driving to the specified meeting point in a buggy. Brazel arrived, from the opposite direction, on horseback.

What happened next remains a mystery, but Brazel apparently shot and killed Garrett. Brazel claimed he fired in self-defence; supporters of Garrett said it was an ambush. Carl Adamson's views were never recorded, but he did take over the lease on the disputed land from Brazel. Read into that what you will!

King George I of Greece (assassinated 18 March 1913)

The reign of George I of Greece lasted from 1863 until his assassination in Thessaloniki in March 1913, just over a year prior to the First World

War. His life and his death were inextricably linked to the ownership of the strategically important island of Crete.

Originally a prince of Denmark, George was educated and intended for a career in the Danish Navy until the Greek National Assembly deposed the unpopular King Otto and elected George to replace him on the throne.

George was still a teenager when he became king, but his accession was supported by all of the main European powers, from the United Kingdom to Russia. His family was exceptionally well-placed, with important links and a wide range of suitable princes and princesses to play the political marriage game. George himself married into the Russian royal family, a connection that turned Czar Nicholas II into his nephew.

His reign lasted for fifty years, making George the longest-serving monarch of Greece. During that time, the country made several important territorial gains. Some, like Thessaly, were annexed from long-time enemies (in this case the Ottomans); others, for example the Ionian Islands, were ceded to Greece by the UK, anxious to create a strong Christian power in the region.

Throughout his reign, George kept up the pressure on the Ottomans, believing that Greek citizens, whoever and whatever they were, should be united in one kingdom.

Unlike his predecessor Otto, King George disliked pomp and ceremony. He was often seen walking in the streets, and would regularly stop to talk with shop owners and passers-by. A 'man of the people', George even ran the last 1,000 yards of the marathon, accompanying the Greek winner of the event in the 1896 summer Olympic Games.

Things began to go wrong for him towards the end of the nineteenth century. The long-running dispute over ownership of Crete culminated in a war with Turkey, one which the Greeks lost. It was a humiliating defeat, after which George's popularity plummeted. Reviled by men and women who had previously supported him, his mind turned to the possibility of abdication.

In 1898, an attempted assassination changed things again. George showed great bravery when his carriage came under fire from two riflemen, placing himself between the gunmen and his daughter, Maria, shielding her with his body. The coachmen and one of the horses were hit, but Maria and George survived the attack. The assassins fled into the hills, where they were hunted down and captured. Both were found guilty of attempted murder and beheaded.

That same year, thanks largely to the influence of the Great Powers – Great Britain, France, Germany, Russia and Austria – Crete was placed under the control of Greece. Despite this success, the next ten years were an unhappy and troubled time for both Crete and Greece. The Young Turk Revolution of 1908 saw the Cretan government, under the direct control of Liberal statesman Eleftherios Venizelos, campaign for unity between Crete and Greece.

Venizelos had become prime minister of the island state. His relationship with King George was always difficult, needing careful handling on both sides. For example, a demand that members of the Greek royal family should be stripped of their military ranks heightened tensions, but George and his sons avoided bloodshed by voluntarily surrendering their commissions. Although tensions continued to be high, the situation remained workable.

In the First Balkan War of 1912, Greece allied itself with Montenegro, Serbia and Bulgaria, fighting against the old enemy, Turkey. The war saw Greece emerge this time as victors. Under Venizelos, now the Greek prime minister, Greece had become a powerful military presence, King George being relegated to what was, more or less, a figurehead position.

Approaching his fiftieth anniversary as king, George began making plans to abdicate. He had done enough, he felt, and his position as monarch was now little more than that of a constitutional figurehead. Such a gesture fitted his personality.

Before he could put these plans into operation, however, on 18 March 1913, George was shot at close range and killed while on his afternoon walk, with no guards or soldiers anywhere in sight. The assassin was

Alexandros Schimas, who claimed to be a socialist, acting on true socialist principles, but was not able to name the party to which he belonged. Six weeks after the assassination, he died, mysteriously falling from a police station window.

Despite the gradual claiming of all real power in Greece by Eleftherios Venizelos, the assassination of George I upset the already shaky balance of power in and around the Mediterranean. With the Balkans in chaos, a weakened Turkey and a rampant Greece, the lines were already being drawn up for the First World War.

Archduke Franz Ferdinand and Sophie, his wife, Sarajevo (assassinated 28 June 1914)

The first decade of the twentieth century had begun quietly enough, but the killing of the heir to the throne of Austria-Hungary, Archduke Franz Ferdinand, in the summer of 1914 was a major contributor to the maelstrom of horror and tragedy that was to become the First World War. The assassination took place in Sarajevo, the capital of Bosnia-Herzegovina, on 28 June 1914.

Throughout the late nineteenth and early twentieth centuries, the Balkan states were a hotbed of violence. As Ottoman influence declined, Serbia, Bosnia and other previously Turkish-dominated states seized on the chance for independence, forming alliances with each other and with major powers like Austria-Hungary. As with any emerging power, however, discontent and disruption were rife.

As early as 1903, Serbian army officers, unhappy with the ruling regime, had stormed the royal palace, pumped thirty pistol bullets into Alexandros, their king, eighteen into his wife, and then flung their naked bodies out of the window – demonstrating only too clearly that that the 'art' of defenestration was not restricted to Prague (where the famous defenestrations of the seventeenth century took place)!

The new dynasty that replaced the assassinated monarch began to move away from links with Austria-Hungary, the traditional ally and supporter of Serbia. It turned, instead, towards Russia.

The population of the Austrian Empire at this time was significantly more Serbian than Austrian, causing major concerns in Vienna. At the same time, economic alliances with Bulgaria and France further antagonized the rulers and statesmen of the Austro-Hungarian Empire. A trade war between Serbia and Austria-Hungary, known as the Pig War, lasted from 1906 until 1909 and did little to help the economy of either nation.

Serbia gradually built up its power and territorial possessions in the region, fighting and winning two Balkan wars in 1912 and 1913. As a result, Macedonia and Kosovo were added to the growing power of Serbia. Bosnia-Herzegovina had been annexed by Austria-Hungary in 1908, with the result that anti-Austrian feelings ran high in all the nations of the region. In Serbia, where anything the Austrians did was now regarded as a challenge, the emotion was particularly virulent.

Austria-Hungary was a dying empire, its decline almost mirroring the gradual toppling of the Ottomans. Nevertheless, that did not stop the aged Emperor Franz Joseph trying to halt his regime's decline, usually with restrictive and reactionary tactics. Unfortunately for him, his powder was damp and emotions continued to run high. This was particularly the case with students and young people, who resented what they saw as high-handed and illegal behaviour on the part of the Austrians.

Revolutionary groups proliferated in almost all of the Bosnian states. One of the many groups operating in Bosnia and Serbia was known as the Young Bosnians, their chant of 'Union or Death' being regularly used to draw people to their flag. Their clearly expressed aim was simple – to free Bosnia-Herzegovina from Austrian overlordship and, in conjunction with Serbia, create a southern Slav state.

Bosnia was at the time a rabid mix of different nationalities. Over half the population were Serbs, a large proportion were Muslims and a slighter smaller group were Croatians. The ethnic mixture made for a potentially aggressive, emotional and dangerous population, one easily moved to violence and public disorder.[7]

Closely linked to the Young Bosnians group of revolutionaries was the Serbian Black Hand Society. This small band of brothers, along with many nationalist groups in Serbia and other Balkan states, was the holder and manipulator of a degree of anger that was far removed from their faintly ludicrous name.

Fanatical, willing to go to any lengths to achieve their aims, the Black Hand's oath of loyalty sums up the serious nature of their motives and of the times in which they operated. Members swore fidelity to the cause on the blood of their ancestors, promising to sacrifice their lives as and when necessary. The Young Bosnians and the members of the Black Hand willingly accepted the challenge of death or success in whatever enterprise they entered upon.

Regardless of the names of their societies – names that were more like gangs from childhood comics than real-life assassination groups – the situation was far from comedic. It was serious stuff. When viewed together, as one unit, the secret societies provided a firm base for revolutionary thought and debate.

The various Balkan secret societies were ideal places for young revolutionaries to 'play' and develop their beliefs, but their very existence made for a more dangerous and deadly force than anyone could imagine. Gavrilo Princip, Nedeljko Cabrinovic and Trifko Grabez, the first three assassins to plot the death of Franz Ferdinand, were all members of the Black Hand and were clear about their purpose:

'At his trial Princip was asked how Bosnia could be freed from Austria and then allowed to join Serbia. His reply was "By terror … killing people at the top, removing those evil doers standing in the way and hindering the idea of unification."'[8]

Gavrilo Princip and the others were not unusual, either in their political leanings or willingness to complete the tasks they adopted. Being a student in the years following the annexation of Bosnia-Herzegovina also meant being a socialist and a revolutionary. Membership of organizations such as the Young Bosnians and the Black Hand was virtually a prerequisite for young men such as Princip.

Fanatical in his belief in Bosnian independence, the 20-year-old Princip often spent whole nights at the grave of Bogdan Zerajic, a radical student who, in 1910, had attempted to kill the Governor of Bosnia-Herzegovina. Zerajic failed and ended his attempt by putting a bullet into his own head. He was exactly the type of martyr and inspiration that young men like Gavrilo Princip needed.

The secret societies went far beyond the provision of forums for debate and argument. They were regularly provided with bombs and guns by people such as Dragutin Dimitrijevic, chief of Serbia's Military Intelligence section. Operating under the nickname of Apis, after the Egyptian bull god, he was a key figure in Serbian and Bosnian opposition to Austria-Hungary.

It was not just a case of handing out weapons. The students and other members of the revolutionary groups were trained by Serbian agents and army officers in how to use those weapons effectively. They may have laboured together under the stigma of ludicrous names, but their intentions and, as it turned out, their actions were deadly.

When it was announced that in the summer of 1915 Archduke Franz Ferdinand would visit Sarajevo to observe Bosnian military manoeuvres, Princip knew that his moment in history had come. He was trained, he was equipped, and he would organize an assassination. He was helped by the fact that Franz Ferdinand's trip would be a relaxed, almost casual visit.

Police presence would be at a minimum, and whatever soldiers were stationed in the country would be engaged in the military manoeuvres. The archduke might proclaim, prior to the visit, 'I would not be surprised if over there a couple of Serbian bullets were waiting for me', but he did not really believe it. Austria-Hungary was still the major player in the region; his uniform and mere presence would deter any revolutionary enterprise.[9]

Franz Ferdinand would be bringing with him his wife, Sophie, Duchess of Hohenberg. The reason for this was simple. Theirs was a Morganatic marriage, Sophie coming from a lower social class than Franz Ferdinand. It was a love match, precedent and position meaning nothing to the pair when they were newlyweds. Only as time went on did the arrangement begin to annoy them:

> 'Sophie could never share his rank, could never share his splendour, could never even sit by his side on any public occasion. There was one loophole – his wife could enjoy the recognition of his rank when he was acting in a military capacity.'[10]

Franz Ferdinand seized this chance to let Sophie enjoy at least some of his glory; a formal occasion where he could parade his wife, as an equal, not ten paces behind him as was so usual. Sophie would love it, and so would he. However, it was the biggest mistake of his life, as Gavrilo Princip was about to prove.

On 28 June 1914, the royal couple left the military manoeuvres and journeyed to Sarajevo by train. They then travelled through Sarajevo in an open-topped car for an official function at the town hall. Almost immediately, they ran into trouble.

Gavrilo Princip had recruited a number of other terrorists, only four of them being particularly active in the plot, but all ready to play their part if needed when the archduke rolled into town. One of the newcomers, Borijove Jevtic, later wrote an account of the assassination, claiming that twenty-two other Bosnians were prowling the streets of Sarajevo that morning, all armed with Browning automatic pistols and grenades. The trials held in the wake of the assassination claimed that there were in fact twenty-five plotters.

In the event, only half a dozen got themselves actively involved with the assassination. Separated at regular 500-yard intervals, the assassins lined the 4-mile length of Appel Quay alongside the Miljacka River. Along this wide street, the archduke and his convoy of cars were to travel, Franz Ferdinand and Sophie in the third vehicle. By some bizarre mistake, what security there was for the convoy saw the police escort crammed into the first car. Franz Ferdinand and Sophie were left virtually unprotected.

The cars travelled slowly, on the orders of the archduke, who wanted the Bosnian crowd to catch a glimpse of himself and Sophie. Meanwhile, each of the killers nervously waited for his opportunity, all the while taking comfort from the fact there was not a policeman or soldier in sight. Soon, the convoy was within range of their guns.

First in line was Muhamed Mehmedbasic, the youngest and least experienced of the seven assassins. That inexperience was to cost him and the other plotters dearly, as, despite Franz Ferdinand's orders, the cars were now moving too quickly and all six of the vehicles were past Muhamed before he realized. It was the same with the second would-be killer.

Third in line was Nedeljko Cabrinovic. With more time to get himself ready, he primed his bomb by smashing it against a lamp-post and hurled it at the archduke's car. The bomb hit the soft lining of the curled-up hood, bounced off and rolled underneath the next car in the convoy. There it exploded, wounding approximately twenty spectators and a number of officials, killing one of them, but leaving Franz Ferdinand unharmed.

Cabrinovic immediately swallowed the cyanide pill he had been given, but it was old and did nothing more than make him sick. He jumped into the river, hoping to drown himself, but after the very hot summer the water was only 13cm deep. Some of the sixty police who were on duty pulled him out, and after a sound beating took him to their headquarters.

The other assassins, perhaps frightened by the explosion, or losing heart and courage, failed to act. Several of them simply gave up and headed for the safety of home.

It was an inept performance all round, and Franz Ferdinand reached the town hall safely. Initially furious, he was calmed down and advised to get out of the city as soon as possible. His proposed journey to the new museum was cancelled.

An alternative route out of Sarajevo, via the hospital for the archduke to see the wounded, was planned. The first two cars would turn off Appel Quay, acting as decoys. Franz Ferdinand and the other cars would carry straight on to the hospital. Unfortunately, nobody had thought to tell Leopold Lojka, the driver of the archduke's car.

Lojka had been ordered only to follow the car in front, so when he saw the first two vehicles turn right, he followed them. The turn half completed, he realized his mistake and came to a halt. And there, Gavrilo Princip was waiting:

'As the car came abreast he stepped forward from the kerb, drew his automatic pistol from his coat and fired two shots. The first struck the Archduchess Sophie in the abdomen. She was an expectant mother. She died (almost) instantly.'[11]

Princip's second shot, like the first one, was totally unaimed, simply loosed off more in hope than design. By sheer luck it hit Franz Ferdinand in the neck. His final words were simple bur heart-rending. 'Don't die, Sophie,' he gasped. 'Live for the children.' It was a forlorn hope. By the time the speeding car arrived at the governor's residence, Sophie was dead, lying at the feet of Franz Ferdinand. Within ten minutes, he too was dead.

Like so many assassinations and events of major significance, rumour, myth and legend soon sprang up around the killing. Gavrilo Princip, it was said, had given up waiting and, feeling hungry, went into a delicatessen on Appel Quay to buy himself a sandwich. He had just finished eating when the archduke's car stopped in front of him.

The consequences of the two assassinations were huge. The killing of the archduke was not, in itself, the cause of the First World War, but it was the spark that ignited tensions and ambitions that had been simmering for years.

Austria-Hungary, Russia and Germany were all soon embroiled in conflict, seizing on the excuse of the archduke's death for a justifiable contest of arms. Like a row of stacked dominoes collapsing one after another, by the end of the summer Austria had declared war on Serbia, Russia on Austria, and Germany on Russia. Even Britain, using the excuse of a long-forgotten treaty protecting Belgium – but in reality afraid of losing its position in the world – was soon embarked on a conflict it did not need but, at the same time, could not afford to ignore.

The First World War resulted in a casualty list of close to 20 million people. It saw the demise of empires and the end of royal, dynastic rule in Russia, Germany and Austria. It was, at the time, the most catastrophic conflict ever to assail mankind.

In light of the war, the punishment of the assassins went almost unnoticed. However, where and when the guilt became clear to everyone, that punishment was severe. Princip, like Cabrinovic, was badly beaten and was lucky to escape with his life, but because of his youth he managed to avoid the death penalty. Sentenced to twenty years in prison, the maximum sentence for any under-age killer in Bosnia or Serbia, he died in 1918 from tuberculosis which had entered his bones.

Other plotters, due to their extreme youth, also escaped the ultimate punishment and suffered similar prison sentences to Princip. Only the distant organizers and planners went to the gallows. There remains something appropriate, a sense of divine intervention, in that simple fact.

Chapter Three

The War Years and a Little More Besides, 1914–1919

The sheer horror of the First World War, its monumental blood-letting on a scale never seen before, rather pushed into the background the concept of assassination, at least for the four years that the war lasted. It did not go away, of course, but unlike so many other recent conflicts in the lead up to what became known as the Great War, the terror of what men (and some women) were forced to endure on the various battle fronts was more than enough to cope with.

Where assassinations did occur, they were part of the greater drama of the war, inextricably linked to the fate of nations. The war, of course, managed to shield many mysterious deaths. There is no figure, no real information, detailing the names and numbers of soldiers killed – assassinated if you like – by their own troops, but it was probably quite significant.

To some extent it remains guesswork, but feudal Russia undoubtedly saw a number of war-weary soldiers turn their weapons on their officers. That was not really a problem with volunteer soldiers, but was so with men like the Russian conscripts who had no choice about when and why they served, those who just obeyed, until the stresses and strains became too much.

It could be argued that the millions of soldiers who were killed in the various battles, wiped out going 'over the top' into a hail of artillery shells and machine-gun bullets, were victims of cold-blooded assassination. Douglas Haig and the other generals would not have considered such a description, not even for a moment, but it is worthy of consideration.

The casualty lists for the first day of the Somme, Passchendaele and the rest would certainly seem to indicate a total lack of concern or care on the part of the generals. 'A good morning's work,' said Haig when told of the 35,000 casualties at the Third Battle of Ypres. If that is not evidence of a deliberate sacrifice or assassination, then I don't know what is!

By the brutality of the deeds, by their significance and relevance to the war and the post-war world, certain assassinations do stand out, however. To begin with, there is the death of the Russian mystic and holy man Rasputin.

Grigori Rasputin, St Petersburg (assassinated 30 December 1916)

There were no half-measures about Grigori Rasputin; people loved him or hated him. In what was really a very short period of time, this outsider from a peasant family in Siberia became a wielder of immense power and influence in Russia. The focus for judgement on that matter is still unclear – was his influence for good or for bad?

The First World War had been raging for two-and-a-half years when a group of aristocrats in the court of Czar Nicholas II of Russia came to the conclusion that his influence was for the bad. The 'mad monk', they decided, had been around long enough. The result was one of the most dramatic assassinations of the twentieth century.

Not unlike the assassination of Franz Ferdinand and its contribution to the start of the First World War, the killing of Rasputin also played a significant part in the history of Russia, even of the world. More than anything, his death signalled the end of the Romanov dynasty, the demise of Imperial Russia and the coming of the communist state and the USSR.

A monk, healer, drunkard and sexual pervert, Rasputin was one of the most controversial figures of the twentieth century. He rarely washed or bathed, slobbered over his food – which he ate without knife or fork – and stank of body odour and bad breath. He had long, lank hair, clothes which should have been discarded years before and manners that were coarse, even crude; on the face of it, there was little that could be termed in any way attractive or appealing to the senses about Rasputin.

And yet he had the ability to charm, to seduce, to bend people to his will. His power over the Russian royal family, Czarina Alexandra in particular, was, even in 1916, legendary across Russia and the whole of Europe.

By 1914, the Russian Bear, long feared by the controllers of other colonial war machines, was an anachronism, an out-of-date power resting uneasily in the hands of the Romanov family. The dynasty and the empire were on their last legs, riven by peasant or working-class factions where men were just beginning to understand their own strength and potential. Class divisions and an aristocratic leadership that belonged in the Middle Ages added to the problems, but the outbreak of war with Germany pushed the Romanovs closer to the edge of disaster.

Czar Nicholas II had assumed leadership of the army early on in the war and was away at the front, leading his armies in one hopeless campaign after another. Running the country was left to the aristocracy, increasingly to the czar's wife, Alexandra. Behind her, pushing and pulling the government first in one unclear direction, then in another, was Grigori Rasputin.

He had come to the notice of the czarina in 1906 when her son, Alexis, a long-term sufferer from haemophilia, was enduring a particularly bad bout of the disease. With internal and external bleeding and gross swellings in various parts of the body, Alexis was in severe pain and Alexandra was distraught.

She and the czar had met Rasputin, in passing, the previous year. Now, however, she heard about the miraculous healing powers of the monk. She would try anything to help her boy, and Rasputin duly arrived at the czar's palace in St Petersburg:

'It is believed that Rasputin's personal charisma relaxed the boy enough so that his body was thus able to improve on its own. Placebo effect? Probably. But to Empress Alexandra, the monk with the unwashed hair and dirty fingernails was a miracle worker.'[1]

From that point on, whenever Alexis was in pain, Rasputin was called in to help. Indeed, he seemed to have free access to the boy and to the luxuries of the royal palace. More importantly, whatever he did to young Alexis seemed to work. His influence was not reserved just for the sick child. As the war went on, Rasputin began to exert more control over the czarina and over the conduct of the conflict. German by birth, Alexandra was already hated by the majority of Russian officials and ordinary citizens. Now Rasputin joined her at the top of the 'hate list'.

The monk soon became so powerful that many of the religious, political and military leaders of the country viewed him as a threat to their own positions. That was fine when things were going well, but from the end of 1915, only military disaster and economic hardship awaited Russia.

Led by Prince Felix Yusupov, a group of five highly placed officials and aristocrats hatched a plan to rid Russia of Rasputin. On the evening of 30 December 1916, lured to the palace of Prince Yusupov by the prospect of a night with the prince's beautiful wife, Rasputin was taken to a downstairs room or cellar and fed with cakes baked by plotter Dr Lazovert. Each of them was covered in enough cyanide to kill at least ten men.

Rasputin is reputed to have survived this, possibly due to the fact that his stomach did not produce the hydrochloric acid needed to activate the poison. It was thus time for Plan B. Filled with panic, Prince Yusupov shot Rasputin in the back. The monk fell screaming to the floor and was pronounced dead. Kicks and punches from Yusupov and the other assassins were delivered with scorn – acts that may have contributed to the monk's revival. He was not yet dead.

As Rasputin began to lash out in rage, and presumably from the pain of his injuries, the assassins fled upstairs. The half-dead victim began to crawl after them up the staircase. He floundered through an outside door and arrived in the snow-covered courtyard. There, Vladimir Purishkevich fired four bullets into the defenceless man. Carried back downstairs to the cellar, Rasputin was beaten with iron bars about the head and chest – just to make sure that 'the man they could not kill' was finally dead.

Wrapped in a curtain, Rasputin's 'corpse' was driven to the Neva River and unceremoniously dumped through a hole in the ice. When the body was later recovered, an autopsy showed that there was water in Rasputin's lungs – proving he had still been alive when he was thrown into the frozen river.[2]

The assassination of Grigori Rasputin did nothing to help either the Russian war effort or the rule of Czar Nicholas II. It was increasingly obvious that Nicholas had neither the aptitude nor the skill to govern the Russian Empire or its army.

Disasters continued, and in March 1917 Nicholas was persuaded to abdicate. In the wake of his departure, Russia pulled out of the war. Peace between Russia and Germany did nothing for the Russian people, but it did free up extra German troops to fight against the Allies on the Western Front.

Mata Hari (assassinated 15 November 1917)

Many people content themselves with the belief that Mata Hari was simply executed for spying activities during the First World War. In fact, her death on 15 November 1917 was quite probably an assassination, an unusual one maybe, but still an ending that was planned and perpetrated by French officials.

At the end of 1916, the French High Command, after the catastrophic losses at Verdun and a number of mutinies in their armies, along with other serious setbacks, were desperately in need of relief. The easiest and quickest way was to find a scapegoat, not to take the blame for the military failures but as a way of showing their efficiency and ability to wage war.

The French had to offer something that would take the attention of the world's press and their unhappy British allies away from what had for them been a pretty hopeless year. And what was better than a beautiful, exotic spy whose name was already renowned across Europe?

If she was indeed a spy, then Mata Hari was probably the most inefficient and inept exponent of espionage in the whole of the twentieth century. In hindsight, it is clear that she was set up, evidence against her twisted until the truth was lost in a web of deceit.

Inevitably, given the strength and standing of her opposition, she was shot by firing squad. The assassins were not the soldiers who pulled the triggers of their rifles but the senior officers of the French military and the various high-ranking government officials who have ever since remained safely anonymous.

Mata Hari, whose real name was Margareta Gertrude Zelle, was born in Holland in 1876. An exotic dancer, high-class call-girl and mistress of many important officials, she was a lot better in the art of sex and seduction than she ever was at spying. Despite this, her name has become a catch-all for beautiful and exotic female spies – indeed, for anyone whose motives and actions might be considered unclear or questionable.

Loving the high life, Mata Hari married an officer in the Dutch colonial service. It was a troubled, even violent relationship, one which took her to the Far East for half-a-dozen years:

'She became fascinated and skilled in the dances of the Far East. Her interpretations of the dances were exactly that, interpretations geared for western eyes and ears, rather than exact reproductions of Eastern art. They thrilled and captivated those who saw them.'[3]

Upon her return to Europe, Mata Hari began to exploit her skills. She also exploited her exotic looks and personality. When war broke out in 1914, she was nearly 40, her looks and talent fading but still able to attract the attention of army officers on leave from the front. In August that year, she was performing in Berlin, her position as a neutral Dutch woman enabling her to move freely around Europe. She charged enormous fees for her services but men were willing to pay simply to say that they had slept with the famous Mata Hari.

Incessant travelling around war-torn Europe might have been exciting, but it also exposed her to accusations of spying. Simply being able to visit one country after another was enough to cause alarm in both German and French camps. When interviewed by British counter-intelligence officers during a trip to London, she freely admitted to having slept with French and German officers, even with various Cabinet officials.

When she came to trial, one of the chief accusations against her was that she had accepted money from both French and German sources, supposedly in an attempt to bribe people such as the German Crown Prince.

This Mata Hari freely admitted, but said that she viewed the substantial sums of money she received as compensation for clothes and props lost when war broke out. She said she had no intention of bribing or influencing anyone. Naïve she certainly was, but nationality and patriotism clearly meant very little to her, even though she openly declared at her trial: 'Harlot, yes; traitor never.'[4]

In 1917, Mata Hari was arrested by the French while in Paris and charged with spying for Germany. There was virtually no proof that she had ever engaged in espionage, most people accepting her story that any money she might have received was no more than gifts from grateful lovers.

The one thing she could not deny or explain away was that a sum of 20,000 francs had been given to her by the German consul in Amsterdam. The money was payment for providing information on French troop movements in the months ahead; in other words, it was for things that had not yet happened. How could she, Mata Hari asked, be accused of things that had not taken place?

Her defence, such as it was, rested mainly on her neutrality. Yes, she had received money from various sources – French and German alike – but she was a courtesan, a high-class whore. Countless other women had been given large sums of money by their lovers; it was expected and accepted by all parties.

She had never betrayed anyone, Mata Hari naively declared, and although she was Dutch by birth, she had always retained a partiality for France. For the French prosecutors, it was simply a question of allowing her to condemn herself.

The result of the trial was a foregone conclusion. Mata Hari was found guilty, and on 15 November 1917 was executed by firing squad. Her courage in the face of death apparently so upset the firing squad that their aim was poor. She was only wounded, having to be finished off by the officer in charge with the traditional bullet in the ear.

Mata Hari may have been a German spy; she may have been a French one. But she was certainly not a good spy, for either side. The Germans later admitted that she had never passed on any useful information to them. But, they declared, the publicity surrounding Mata Hari's trial and execution had been very useful to them.

Arrest and trial in Britain or Germany would probably have shown her to be naïve in her behaviour but innocent of spying. Mata Hari's misfortune was that everything – arrest, trial and execution – took place in a country which required an example to be set, where the populace needed to be warned of the dangers of subverting the structure and morale of the nation. It was a clear case of wrong place, wrong time.

Czar Nicholas II and the Russian Royal Family, Yekaterinburg, Siberia (assassinated 17 July 1918)

Unwillingly and unhappily called back from the Eastern Front in the early days of 1917, Czar Nicholas Alexandrovich Romanov, Emperor of Russia, found his country in utter chaos. The cost of food was at an all-time high and rioting in the cities had become common.

Over 1.7 million Russian soldiers had died in the war, perhaps another million civilians, and now even the guards who were supposed to defend the czar, his family and his palaces were in a state of open rebellion. Mutiny in the garrison at Petrograd was threatening to overwhelm the entire country. The situation was desperate, even hopeless.

Czar Nicholas II formally abdicated as Emperor of Russia on 2 March 1917, knowing that he would then have to go into exile. His original intention was to leave the throne in favour of his son, Alexis, but medical advice soon declared that the young boy would be lucky to survive twelve months in such a perilous position without family support.

A second option was to leave everything to the Grand Duke Michael, brother of Nicholas. Michael refused to accept the throne, however, until a Constituent Assembly voted either for the continuation of the monarchy or the establishment of a republic. His appointment was deferred and a provisional government under Alexander Kerensky assumed control.

Nicholas has been a figure of debate ever since his abdication, opinion falling into two distinct groupings. Was he a victim of the time and of circumstance, or was he simply an inept exponent of tyrannical dictatorship? There are still historians who describe him as 'Bloody Nicholas', but that position has been weakened somewhat over recent years:

> 'Most commonly he is described as shallow, weak, stupid … Historians admit that Nicholas was a good man but personal factors are irrelevant; what matters is that Nicholas was a "bad Czar."'[5]

He had not wanted to be czar, and was certainly never trained for the position. By nature an autocrat, Nicholas inherited a Russia that was fractured and splintering apart. It would have taken a very able man to hold the country together, let alone mend it. But Nicholas Romanov was certainly not the man for the job. Arguably, when the time came to leave it all behind, he was relieved.

Upon abdication, his first thought was not for his country but to establish safety and security for his family and himself. Theoretically, that should have been easy enough to obtain. Both George V of England and Kaiser Wilhelm of Germany were first cousins. Other influential relatives included King Haakon of Norway and Christian X of Denmark. One of them, surely, would offer help?

However, no help was forthcoming. For a brief while, it seemed that George V and England might offer sanctuary, but that was soon halted by the machinations of Prime Minister David Lloyd George and left-wing elements in Parliament. It was felt to be better all round for the deposed czar to go to a neutral country. Friendship and support of the new Menshevik government in Russia was more important than the fate of the czar.

Nicholas next appealed to France for help, but the same chaotic emotions that had sent Mata Hari to her grave meant that French help was not available. Germany, as the enemy that had played a major role in bringing about the czar's downfall, was never an option.

Nicholas and his family, along with a doctor and some servants, were held first in Tobolsk, but later in 1917 they were moved to the remote Siberian town of Yekaterinburg. There, they were imprisoned in the two-storey Ipatiev House, a building also known by the haunting and threatening appellation of 'the house of special purpose'.[6]

By the beginning of 1918, the Russian Civil War was raging. White Russian forces, supporters of the czarist regime aided by troops from most of the Allied nations, were pushing hard at Leon Trotsky's newly formed Red Army, forcing them back inland. By March, they were just a day or so away from Yekaterinburg and rescue of the royal family appeared to be a distinct possibility.

The Bolshevik government, created after the October/November Revolution the previous year, had always intended putting Nicholas on trial for numerous crimes against the Russian people. Now, the rapid advance of White Russian units, along with the exposure of a failed plot to free the czar and his family, forced their hand.

The Presidium of the Ural Regional Soviet, fulfilling what was described as the will of the people, decided that no trial was needed. The czar would be assassinated. Preparation was painstaking. Materials to saturate and burn the bodies, guns to actually carry out the killing and a team of assassins were all gradually put into place.

In the early summer of 1918, Yakov Yurovsky, the officer in charge of the czar's 'prison', was told to hold himself in readiness and await the word from Moscow. That word was not long in coming.

The imperial family, along with their servants, were awakened in the early hours of 17 July and ushered into a basement cellar. The firing squad, armed with hand guns, assembled in an adjacent room. Nicholas and the others settled into armchairs and waited.

As soon as the formal and final approval came, Yakov Yurovsky informed Czar Nicholas that he and his family would be shot. The czar's response was one of disbelief. 'What?' he stuttered. 'What did you say?' Then the firing began. Nicholas was the first to die, shot several times in his chest and body – not in the head, as has sometimes been claimed.

Myths and legends about the assassinations began almost immediately. Most of them were false. For example, it was rumoured that the czar's four daughters – Anastasia, Tatiana, Olga and Maria – had sewn diamonds and other valuables into their petticoats. These acted as bullet proof protection. It is a great story, but totally untrue. They may well have sewn in jewels, but they were never intended and certainly not used as protection from gunfire.

Alexis, it was said, held himself erect, as protection between his father and the gunmen. Again, not true. He probably died in his father's arms. The gunfire was always said to be accurate. Well, maybe so, but smoke from the weapons clouded the air in the cellar and the final breaths of the royal family were snatched away by bayonets, fists and boot heels.

The most lasting story, however, is that two of the victims, Alexis and one of his sisters, probably Anastasia, escaped the shooting. That legend survived until 2007, imposters and claimants regularly pushing forward their case for recognition. Discovery of all the bodies, thrown down a disused mineshaft, and the use of DNA ended the speculation for ever.

The decision to assassinate Czar Nicholas II was a monumental move on the part of Vladimir Lenin and the Bolshevik government. It did not hurt Lenin unduly, although it did manage to push the czar's abdication off the front pages of the newspapers for a while. Even so, a small cadre of pro-monarchy supporters, underground and secret, came into existence. They are still present in Russia today.

The assassinations cannot have been unexpected by the governments of the West. They trotted out the usual formal complaints, but nothing else was done. In time, Lenin was succeeded by Stalin, the communist regime went its own way and, eventually, the Cold War ensured that the empires of the East and West would remain distinctly different units. Who knows what might have happened if Nicholas had lived.

Rosa Luxemburg and Karl Liebknecht, Berlin (assassinated 15 January 1919)

The assassination of German communist leaders Rosa Luxemburg and Karl Liebknecht in January 1919 was an event that summed up the chaos and confusion of post-First World War Germany.

Karl Liebknecht was born in Leipzig. A determined socialist, he had served as a Deputy in the Reichstag from 1912 until 1916 before quitting the Social Democratic Party to found the more dynamic and outspoken Spartacus League.

Rosa Luxemburg, co-founder of the Spartacus League alongside Liebknecht, was Polish by birth but had taken German citizenship in 1897. One of Germany's first women Doctors of Law, she was as committed to left-wing politics as Liebknecht. A confirmed Marxist, Rosa was also vehemently anti-war.

Both Karl and Rosa became key figures in the revolutionary socialist groups that sprang up in Germany in the wake of the country's defeat in the Great War. Previously, Germany had always been an autocratic, right-wing country. However, military defeat and the enforced abdication of Kaiser Wilhelm II left Germany without any form of familiar leadership, thus creating a so-called democracy out of what had been, effectively, a military junta.

The Treaty of Versailles, perhaps the most ill-judged peace treaty in history, had helped create an impoverished and poorly led nation. The Weimar Republic – a republic without a republican, as was once declared – was left to battle with insurgent groups, a crippled economy and policies that were little more than watching people jump from one crisis point to the next.

It was a dangerous time, murder and killing often emerging as an alternative to responsible government and leadership. People like Rosa Luxemburg and Karl Liebknecht were open targets for the right-wing groups that challenged their Spartacus League. Anti-League posters and handbills declaring 'Beat their leaders – Kill Liebknecht' were common in Berlin and other cities.[7]

Both Rosa and Karl spent the last two-and-a-half years of the war in prison because of their views and actions, but upon their release they immediately revitalized and reorganized the Spartacus League. Founding the newspaper *The Red Flag* gave them access to similar groups in all parts of the country. It was perhaps inevitable that death and disaster would soon arrive.

The Spartacus Rising of 1918 was a full-scale rebellion against the Weimar Republic, leading to open warfare on the streets of Berlin. Rosa Luxemburg was opposed to the rising, but once it began she felt she had no alternative other than to support the actions of her comrades. Despite her misgivings, she threw herself into backing the rising, declaring: 'Today we can seriously set about destroying capitalism for once and for all.'

The revolt was put down, brutally and without mercy, by Freikorps irregulars employed by Frederick Ebert, Chancellor of the Weimar government. Ebert was a man who had once been a student of Rosa Luxemburg, lending an air of unreality to events. More than thirty Spartacists were killed and by 11 January 1919 it was all over. Not for Rosa Luxemburg and Karl Liebknecht, however.

Both Rosa and Karl were forced to go into hiding, but someone, unknown and never identified, betrayed their whereabouts. On 15 January, a 'hit squad' of battle-hardened Freikorps fighters stormed into the house where they were hiding and dragged them off into custody.

Raw hatred appeared to be central to the action by the Freikorps, but that was not their only reward. Each member of the arresting squad received a gift of 1700 marks from the civic council, blood money that was easily found. Both Rosa and Karl must have known what fate awaited them.

Once in custody, the two Spartacist leaders were separated from each other. Rosa was tortured while instructions were sought from the local government. It took some time for those in authority to make a decision, but in the end the message was simple: 'You know what to do.'

Rosa was immediately smashed to the floor with a rifle butt, then shot once in the back of the head. Her body was dumped unceremoniously into the nearby Landwehr Canal.

Karl was also tortured before being taken to the Tiergarten Park, where he was shot many times. The assassins, members of the Guard Rifle Division, then took his lifeless body and threw it into the street at the entrance to the Berlin Zoo.

The discarding of the bodies in such careless and disrespectful fashion was deliberately done. It was the final stage of a carefully planned assassination where, in the eyes of the right-wing assassins, the victims were no better than dead animals.

Idealized by many as communist martyrs, Rosa Luxemburg and Karl Liebknecht became symbols of sacrifice for a cause. Luxemburg, in particular, achieved in her death a degree of fame she could never have hoped to obtain in life. Books were written about her, statues and memorials erected. For many communist supporters, Rosa became a figure to cling to in the coming fragile years of the Nazi Party and Stalin's ferocious period of destruction.

The writer Berthold Brecht commemorated her in a poem that was set to music by Kurt Weill. Simple in style and content, it captures the mood of the time and the inevitability of Rosa's end:

> 'Red Rosa now has vanished too,
> And where she lies is hid from view.
> She told the poor what life's about
> And so the rich have rubbed her out.'[8]

It is a simple enough piece of verse by one of Germany's greatest writers, but Rosa Luxemburg would probably have been content with it.

Emiliano Zapata (assassinated 10 April 1919)

One of the most original and renowned of all twentieth-century revolutionaries, Mexican hero Emiliano Zapata was also a man of dedication and drive. His life and adventures, wonderfully portrayed on the silver screen by Marlon Brando, still make superb viewing, but give only a brief glimpse of the full story.

Zapata was of mixed race, a *mestizo*, as he and others like him were known. He was born in 1879 in the small town of Morelos, which, thanks to its sugar-growing industry, was one of the richest areas of Mexico. None of that wealth came to Zapata or his family, however, as Mexican society was brutally uneven, most of the land and industry in the country being held and exploited by a small minority of rich landowners.

Always interested in politics, in particular the possibility of land reform, almost as soon as he came of age, Zapata was elected head of his village. He was young and vibrant, determined to make a better life for his people. If necessary, he would do this by force.

A great lover of women, Zapata was always conscious of his appearance. He invariably wore tight silver-buttoned trousers and a wide sombrero, an outfit that made him instantly recognizable to everyone. Elegant and striking with his thick moustache, he was hugely popular with the women of Mexico, who awarded him almost godlike status.

In 1910, revolution broke out in the country, a conflict in which Zapata eagerly took part. The revolt culminated in the deposition of the long-serving President Diaz, but in the opinion of Zapata and many others who had fought in the war, Francisco Madero, his replacement, was not much better.

Zapata fought on against Madero and was soon in command of a small rebel army, a formation that eventually grew to 20,000 in number. At the height of his power, he controlled almost one-third of Mexico, helping to depose one president after another.

By clever use of blackmail – threatening to burn crops and buildings unless he was paid off – he managed to force the wealthy landowners of the country to finance his Liberation Army of the South. It was sweet poetic justice, Zapata felt.

In April 1919, while fighting yet another president, Zapata was contacted by Venustiano Carranza, one of the government's leading soldiers. He had had enough of the country's ruler and was, Carranza said, ready to defect along with his troops. A meeting was arranged at a hacienda in Zapata's home town of Morelos, both Carranza and Zapata agreeing to leave the majority of their troops behind and bring with them a personal bodyguard of just thirty men.

However, Carranza arrived at the meeting on 10 April with 600 well-armed and vengeful soldiers. Coming face to face with Zapata, they immediately opened fire from point-blank range. Zapata was riddled with bullets and died instantly.

His body was then dragged by a mule through the dirt and desert streets of Morelos. The chief assassin and designer of the plot, Carranza, was paid a huge sum for Zapata's body and promoted to general.

Following his assassination, Zapata's army soon dissolved, although many supporters refused to believe he was actually dead. It was, they claimed, a lookalike or a doppelganger who had been shot down in his place. Only gradually did the reality of the situation hit home for Zapata's Mexican supporters.

Zapata might have been dead, but his name lived on. Streets, even whole towns, were named after him, and his face soon appeared on Mexican banknotes.

Although Emiliano Zapata was not there to see them, many of the land reforms he had wanted so badly and fought so desperately to achieve actually came into existence in the two decades after the First World War.

Pancho Villa, Mexican, Mexico (assassinated 20 July 1923)

Born into poverty, Pancho Villa rose to a position where he was as powerful and effective a revolutionary as Mexico's other bandit hero, Emiliano Zapata. Villa controlled the north of the country, Zapata the south, and while they occasionally fought against each other, they also came together to oust Mexico's President Huerta in 1914.

In 1902, as a young man, Pancho Villa was captured and sentenced to death for his bandit crimes. Nevertheless, a contact, a man who often bought stolen mules off him, managed to get him a reprieve. As payback, Villa agreed to join the army, but in the space of twelve months he had killed an unpopular officer and deserted. It was back to the old way of life for Pancho.

The Mexican Revolution of 1910 saw him fighting against President Diaz until one of the generals, who saw him as a threat, had him arrested and charged with murder and revolutionary activities. Villa escaped and spent the next few years fighting Mexican government soldiers and occasionally raiding American territory across the border.

The highpoint of Villa's career came in 1914 when he drove President Carranza out of Mexico City. Events after that followed something of a downward trend for Pancho.

A number of heavy defeats saw him retire from banditry, taking up the offer of a pension from the president. However, he kept up his revolutionary involvement. There were rumours that his units were, in the final stages of the First World War, funded by the German government. The US government even sent army units into Mexico to chase him away, but without success.

An inveterate womaniser, Villa had numerous relationships and godchildren all over the country. On his way to the christening of one of these, he drove directly into an ambush. As the ambushers were about to open fire, children from a nearby school poured out at the end of their day of studies. The assassins held their fire.

Two weeks later, on 20 July 1923 at the same roadway point, Pancho Villa was not so lucky. Passing a street vendor, he and his bodyguards heard the shout, 'Viva Villa'. It was a signal to open fire.

Seven gunmen fired on Villa's car, hitting him nine times and killing him instantly. Others in the car also died in the ambush. The assassination seems to have had some form of official or government backing, but the cause has never been fully explained. President Carranza had returned to power and certainly had a grudge against Villa, so his involvement remains a possibility.

Chapter Four

A Short but Bloody Interlude, 1920–1929

The ten or so years between 1918 and 1930 saw a frantic and frenetic period in world history. The era which followed the signing of the Treaty of Versailles in 1919 was symbolized not just by a sense of rapturous peace and hope for the future, but by the direct opposite – a number of mass killings and assassinations.

In many respects, it was as if the barbarity and the bloodletting, the sheer cruelty of a war like nobody had ever seen before, had not been enough. In just over four years, men on all sides of the conflict had come face to face with death, many of them not surviving. Bombs, shells, mud and machine guns – there was no escape from the rigours and methods of modern warfare. Soldiers suffered and died in their hundreds of thousands.

In the eyes of many, the assassination of a few dozen more victims, despite what was supposed to be an era of peace and celebration, hardly registered. If the war had taught the world anything, it was simply that men – and women – were replaceable.

In one way or another, the Treaty of Versailles which ended the First World War also ended many longstanding but obviously out-of-date and semi-derelict empires. In the years to come, major players in world politics like Austria-Hungary, Germany, Russia and Turkey were all forced to re-examine their structures and their status.

It was time for colonial possessions in areas such as the Middle East and Africa to look again at the structures which had kept them tethered to what had been, for generations past, significant Western overlords. Exploitation of people and resources had been masked for too long by protestations and proclamations of goodwill towards what were really little better than slaves. In 1919, it was clear that the old fall-back of 'muscular Christianity' was dead and buried – but not forgotten.

Incidents such as the 1919 massacre at Amritsar in India resonate even now. The massacre was a truly horrific and unnecessary event, in which somewhere between 500 and 1,500 Indians were shot by Brigadier General Dyer and his British Indian Army troops. These killings at the Jallianwala Bagh in the Punjab region of India, which destroyed the lives of innocent passers-by as well as protestors, were not assassinations but sheer murder, with little or no aim or purpose.

In a relatively short space of time, without warning or provocation, men, women and children were mown down for no apparent reason. The names and identities of the dead did not matter to the Gurkha mercenaries and British soldiers who carried out the shootings.

Obviously it was not the only cause, but the Amritsar massacre was a significant element in a process of soul-searching that eventually ended with Indian independence and the winding up of the British Empire. There were many other incidents, perhaps not so bloody nor so significant, but they also remained fixed in the memory of millions of natives.

In their own way, unlike the visitation of 'death in the afternoon' at Amritsar, the majority of the killings were assassinations and were all influential in creating an environment where it was, if not acceptable, then at least understandable to reach for the gun as something of a first resort in time of crisis. Macrocosm or microcosm, mass assassination had become more important than ever before.

For Britain, of course, there was an ever-present problem right on its own doorstep, in the dissatisfied island of Ireland. The Easter Rising of 1916 and the subsequent execution of fourteen of the republican rebels, one so badly wounded he could not stand and was shot tied to a chair, had effectively created martyrs and further fuelled the Irish independence movement.

In the 1920s, after having been held in check by the war, the problem exploded in outbreaks of violence by the Irish Republican Army, incidents that shocked the whole world.

The Cairo Gang, Dublin (multiple assassinations on 21 November 1920)

The Cairo Gang was one of several nicknames given to a group of British intelligence agents, serving out of uniform, sent to Dublin during the Irish War of Independence. Mostly demobbed soldiers, augmented by members of the Irish Constabulary, they arrived as a group in January 1920 after training delivered by MI5 in London and at other locations. Their express aim was identifying, targeting and then killing members of the IRA.

The group was sometimes known as D Branch, the name springing from their official title, the Dublin District Special Branch. It is not clear where the appellation of the Cairo Gang originated. One explanation is that the men had a common history of serving together in the Middle East, but it is more likely to be something less official: on most evenings, the group gathered together in the Cafe Cairo in Grafton Street, and their regular use of the cafe probably gave the group its name.

The Cafe Cairo meetings were informal and fairly rowdy, filled with gossip and tall tales. Inevitably, the regularity of the meetings and a general lack of security furnished the IRA with useful information about the habits and practices of British intelligence officers.

The result was that Michael Collins, Director of Intelligence for the IRA, carefully and meticulously prepared an assassination plot. It was the opening salvo in a day-long wave of killings, soon to be known as Bloody Sunday, on 21 November 1920.

Collins had created a highly effective intelligence system which kept him well informed and provided a great deal of vital information. This ranged from idle gossip gleaned by customers in the Cafe Cairo to more crucial and reliable facts from double agents supposedly working for the British, but in reality reporting straight back to Collins.

The range of informants was vast, from mock informers who were really IRA operatives, to domestic staff working in the lodgings of the British, and even policemen and auxiliaries whose true affiliation lay with the Republican forces. Even though they did not know it, the Cairo Gang soon found themselves out of their league in a deadly game of espionage. Put simply, they were outgunned, outthought and outmanoeuvred.

On the other hand, thanks to the deadly genius of Michael Collins, the IRA was well in control. It meant that when the IRA was ready to strike, its members knew almost everything they needed to know about their enemy – their addresses, their routines, everything.

The assassinations were conducted on an individual basis, house by house, victim by victim, beginning at 9.00 am on 21 November.

The IRA killers, known as The Squad, entered six different houses in various locations across Dublin, sometimes with the aid of sledgehammers to batter down the doors, and killed fourteen members of the Cairo Gang. One more died from his wounds later in the day, while a further five were seriously wounded.

Hotels such as the imposing and popular Gresham in the centre of Dublin were also targeted. IRA members pretending to be British soldiers arrived at the Gresham with 'important messages' for their officers. Directed to their rooms, they shot and killed two British soldiers as they opened their hotel bedroom doors.

The 'hit squad' approach was not always a success, however. In the Eastwood Hotel, The Squad failed to find their targets and the British agents managed to escape with their lives.

As with any delicate operation, there were moments of bravery and of mistakes. Lieutenant Colonel Hugh Morgan Wood, not a member of the Cairo Gang, was dressed in full military uniform as he left his lodgings to take a formal parade that morning. Coming face to face with the assassins, he turned and shouted a warning to the other residents. Despite being shot in the back, he survived.

Several Cairo Gang members, along with informers, were found at 119 Morehampton Road. Asking not to be shot in front of their wives, they were taken to an empty bedroom, where they were executed. One man, the brother-in-law of one of the officers, escaped the coup and fled to Scotland.

Captain Newberry and his wife were in bed at 92 Lower Baggot Street when they heard the front door being smashed open. They barricaded themselves into their room, but Newberry was shot dead as he tried to escape out of the window.

In the case of Captain John Crawford, he was captured in his hotel in Fitzwilliam Square. It was decided not to shoot him, as his name was not on the list that had been so carefully prepared by Michael Collins – that was understandable, as he was not a member of the Cairo Gang, just the man in charge of motor repairs for the army. He was given twenty-four hours to leave the country.

Captain Patrick McCormack was shot by mistake. A British Army veterinary surgeon, he was in Dublin simply to buy horses and had nothing to do with the Cairo Gang. Michael Collins later acknowledged this and apologized for his assassination.[1]

Only one IRA man, Frank Teeling, was captured during the actual assassinations. Sentenced to hang for his part in the affair, Teeling had the last laugh when he managed to escape from custody.

Two other assassins were later apprehended and executed. Those members of the Cairo Gang who did not die in the morning raids quickly fled to Dublin Castle for sanctuary or took the next boat back to England.

The destruction of the Cairo Gang was a major success for the IRA, but the real skill of the operation rested with Michael Collins. It was an undoubted setback for the British forces in Ireland.

The Igoe Gang

In the wake of the Cairo Gang disaster, learning from their mistakes and attempting to bring their intelligence work up to the standard of Michael Collins, the British forces developed what soon became known as the Igoe Gang.

The Identification Branch of the Combined Intelligence Service, named Igoe after Head Constable Eustace Igoe, took the fight to the IRA. And in this they were remarkably successful.

Made up of men from the Royal Irish Constabulary, members of the Igoe Gang came from different parts of Ireland. They did exactly what the Cairo Gang was supposed to do, patrolling the streets of Dublin looking for wanted men. They operated out of uniform and did not repeat the mistake of the Cairo Gang by regularly meeting in the same place.

They were often guilty of using excessive force when making arrests, but the Igoe Gang was never penetrated by Collins and his band of informers.

Bloody Sunday, Dublin (multiple assassinations, 21 November 1920)

Ireland's Bloody Sunday had begun with the assassination and elimination of the Cairo Gang early on the morning of 21 November 1920. Revenge was in the air, however, and some form of retaliation from the British was to be expected. Yet nobody expected it would come so soon.

A Gaelic Football match between Dublin and Tipperary was planned to take place at Croke Park in Dublin later on that Sunday afternoon. In light of the morning's events, it was a gathering of the public, most of them innocent parties in the civil war, that the authorities hoped would calm things down.

Perhaps more importantly, they also hoped it would provide them with the opportunity to arrest and eliminate would-be rebels. It was thought that maybe even some of those who had carried out the assassination of the Cairo Gang earlier in the day would be present at the game. It was, though, a risk.

The football match would thus go ahead, it was decided. It was simply too late to cancel or postpone it now, and even if it had been called off, such an action would probably have caused riots all over the city. However, in the wake of the Cairo Gang killings, the army and police decided that they needed to be particularly watchful where large gatherings such as this were concerned.

In the end, 'watchful' was hardly the best description of their actions. The Croke Park football game was many things, but it was never going to be watchful. Indeed, it was outright murder and assassination.

The plan was for the spectators to be monitored by the hated Black and Tans (unemployed former British soldiers recruited into the Royal Irish Constabulary), along with members of the regular British Army and auxiliaries. They would cordon off section after section of the crowd as they arrived at the ground, conduct search operations, then move onto the next group.

Given the earlier assassinations of so many members of the Cairo Gang, feelings amongst the British troops and law enforcers were running high. It was perhaps inevitable that things would go wrong.

Without warning and seemingly without clear provocation, the British troops suddenly opened fire on the spectators and on the football players. The fact that some of the assassins were apparently working off a list seems to indicate that the authorities knew who they were looking for. However they are examined, the killings were a case of assassination rather than massacre or murder.

Fourteen civilians were killed, with sixty more wounded and injured. Three of the dead were children or young adults. William Robertson, the first to be shot, was a teenager, perched up in a tree in order to get a better view of the game. Another of the victims was a bride-to-be, her marriage scheduled for a few days' time. Some accounts declare that several of those shot at the football ground later died from their wounds, bringing the death toll to over thirty. The official death toll, however, remains fourteen.

The killings did not stop at Croke Park. Later that evening, two known IRA men, along with an innocent civilian, were apprehended in the streets of Dublin. They were beaten up by British troops and then dragged to Dublin Castle, where they were shot dead.

According to witnesses, the whole of the Bloody Sunday massacre was unprovoked. Even the two military inquiries that were called to investigate the shootings found that the firing was indiscriminate and excessive. The army was absolved of blame, however, the fault being laid at the door of the Dublin policemen, in particular the Black and Tans.

It is impossible not to see shades of the Amritsar massacre in the events of Bloody Sunday. Like had happened in Amritsar, the assassinations – in this case retaliation killings for the Cairo Gang debacle – further fuelled the independence cause and turned Irish support further and further away from the British.

Bloody Night, Portugal (multiple assassinations, 21 October 1921)

By the end of the First World War, in which it had played a relatively minor role, Portugal's position as a major power had long gone. Like Spain, its nearest neighbour, Portugal had been relegated to second-class status, and what influence the country still clung to was based around trade and the few African colonies it had managed to retain.

Portugal underwent massive political and social disruption during the final years of the nineteenth and early days of the twentieth centuries. This culminated in 1908 with the assassination of King Carlo I and Luis Filipe, the heir apparent.

In the struggle to form and manage a workable regime, the first Portuguese Republic was created in 1910, inspired by and modelled on the Third French Republic of 1870.

Along with the chaos of ridding itself of the monarchy and the creation of a democratic constitution, the country also witnessed an evening of organized political assassination. Known in Portuguese as *Noite Sangrenta*, Portugal's Bloody Night took place in Lisbon during the evening and night of 21 October 1921.

During the day, Prime Minister Antonio Granja, in the face of a parliamentary coup, had found it impossible to sustain his Liberal Party in government. He knew that he would have to resign, something that would once again throw the country into chaos.

President Antonio Jose de Almedia, an old-fashioned traditionalist, was hesitant in appointing a successor government to the Republican Party. He delayed making a decision and in this he was partly responsible for the bloodshed which followed.

Granja had been made prime minister only a few months before, following his successful showing in the country's elections. It was the first time since the Portuguese Republic had been formed that the Democratic Party was not in power, and Almedia believed that they still did not have sufficient support to successfully run the country.

Right or wrong, it was a fatal decision. As darkness fell across the streets of Lisbon, rioting began. Central to this was the 'ghost truck' under the command of one Abel Olimpio, which roared around the city streets with the intention of killing notable dignitaries. First to fall was Prime Minister Antonio Granja.

He was found hiding in the house of a friend and was in the process of being taken off to prison for confinement and trial when the assassins changed their minds. Dragged out of the 'ghost truck', Granja was made to stand on a bridge near the Navy Arsenal and shot in the neck. His lifeless corpse was then shot again, repeatedly, and mutilated by sword thrusts.

Radicals in the Democratic Party had been planning this revolt since they were voted out of office earlier in the year. Central to their plans were the Portuguese Navy and the National Republican Guard. Led by Colonel Manuel Coelho, units of both military arms now marched up the Avenida de Liberdade and, supported by light artillery, took up positions in the Eduardo VII Park.

Sunrise was the signal for the artillery and naval ships moored in the River Tagus to open fire on the government buildings. Metaphorically, and perhaps literally, the government promptly threw up their hands in panic. President Almedia found himself without a government or Prime Minister for the length of what became a very long day.

Six notable figures from the Portuguese government and within the general field of politics had been killed by the operatives of the 'ghost truck, one more being seriously wounded.[2]

Over the next few months, three stand-in prime ministers, none of them particularly secure or happy in the position, took up the role. Elections were postponed on four separate occasions because of the violence in the streets, Portuguese voters finally going to the polls in January 1922. It might be surprising or it might have been expected, but the Democratic Party was returned to power.

Michael Collins, County Cork, Ireland (assassinated 22 August 1922)

If there is one figure of real status and significance to emerge from the troubles in post-war Ireland, it has to be Michael Collins. He was, by turns, brutal, clever, compassionate and determined, and proved himself to be the significant difference between the floundering representatives of the British Government and the dedicated Republican figures from Ireland.

Born in 1890 in the rural heartland of County Cork, Collins's first foray off the farm came when, aged just 15, he moved to London in 1906 to work for the PO Savings Bank. In London, he became a member of the Gaelic Athletic Association, a sports organization with clear political connections and links to other groups such as the Gaelic League and the Irish Brotherhood. He lived for ten years on the outskirts of London before eventually returning to his native Ireland.

He returned to a much-troubled land. The Irish problems in the post-war period have been well documented, but even so they remain confused and confusing. Opinions and objectives amongst the Irish nationalists varied at different times as allegiances changed and altered.

Put simply, the Catholic population of the south, particularly around Cork, wanted independence and a situation where they were totally free from British influence. The mainly Protestant occupiers of Ulster in the north wanted to remain within the British Empire. Both elements were prepared to fight to the death to achieve their aims.

A brilliant organizer and confirmed Irish nationalist, Michael Collins rose steadily in the ranks of the Irish Republican organizations. During the Easter Rising of 1916, he fought alongside renowned figures like James Connoly. When the General Post Office where insurgents were holding out fell to the British, he was taken prisoner along with many other rebels. He was lucky to escape execution, being sent to the Frongoch Internment Camp in North Wales.

Collins's stay in the prison camp was short. Released in December 1916, he was soon promoted to various senior positions within the Republican hierarchy. During the War of Independence in post-Great War Ireland, he served as Director of Intelligence in the Irish Republican Army and then became a government minister in the self-declared Irish Republic.

In 1921, Collins was one of the Irish delegates at the London conference to decide on Ireland's future. Weeks of debate saw only an inability to find a workable solution to what was clearly an insolvable problem. Eventually, British Prime Minister David Lloyd George issued what was really little more than an ultimatum – accept what is being offered or we return to a state of war.

Reluctantly, Collins and the other delegates accepted the British offer. What it came down to was a divided Ireland: Ulster and six counties of the north to remain British, with the remaining twenty-six counties to be given Dominion status. Significantly, members of the newly independent state were to swear allegiance to the British crown.

For the diehard Republicans, the Anglo-Irish Treaty signed in December 1921 was not a political victory but a bitter blow. Division of the country and swearing an oath of loyalty to the British crown were, they felt, tantamount to betrayal. Collins left London uttering his famous final judgement on the situation, the words ringing in the ears of everyone who heard it: 'I have signed my own death warrant.'

He was right. Civil war erupted, and as commander-in-chief of the National Army, Collins was immediately involved, fighting against former comrades. To begin with, being largely against any form of co-operation with Britain, the anti-Treaty supporters had a numerical superiority and the IRA achieved considerable domination. The Munster Republic, with its centre in Cork, lay securely inside a defensive line that stretched across Ireland, running from the rugged west coast to Wexford in the east.

Collins's National Army was poorly trained and outnumbered by the anti-Treaty Republicans. It needed time to become a cohesive entity. Equipped with British weapons, this is what they eventually achieved.

By 1922, it appeared as if the Irish Civil War was winding down. Although the IRA was still fighting fiercely, the pro-Treaty Free State was now in control of most of the country. Michael Collins began a series of visits or inspection trips to recently recovered areas. When he announced that he would visit Cork, both the city and its environs, he was advised not to go as the area was still a hotbed of IRA activity. Collins was adamant. He would make the trip.

On 22 August, he set out for a tour of West Cork, travelling in an open-topped car, painted bright yellow, and escorted by a motorcycle patrolman and an armoured car. At the crossroads of Beal na Blath, the convoy stopped to ask for directions from a man standing outside Long's Pub. Unknown to Collins and his party, the man was a sentry keeping watch over the crossroads while a meeting of high-ranking IRA officers took place inside the pub.

When Collins's party moved on, the IRA devised an impromptu assassination. They knew that the convoy would have to return through Beal na Blath as they had recently blown up a bridge on the only other way back to Cork. They waited in a lane that ran above and parallel to the main road – and kept on waiting all afternoon.

When they were just about to give up and go home, the convoy returned. It was now just past 7.30 pm. Protected by a grassy bank running alongside the lane, and with the road below them blocked by a hastily positioned hay cart, the assassins immediately opened fire.

Emmet Dalton, Free State commander for Cork, who was travelling with Collins, urged the driver of their car to 'Drive like Hell'. Collins declared that escape was the last thing on in his mind. They would stop and fight.

When it appeared that Collins and his men were winning the combat, the IRA soldiers began to pull back. His blood up, Collins jumped out of cover behind the armoured car, running around the corner of the road in an attempt to get himself on the flank of the assailants, when he was shot in the back of the head. He was dead almost immediately.

It was later claimed that the fatal shot was fired by Denis O'Neill, formerly a sniper in the British Army. He was given an award by the Republican State, but quite how true the allegation really was remains unknown.

Impulsive and dynamic to the end, the death of Michael Collins was a needless sacrifice. The assassins were pulling back, the ambush as good as over and nobody needed to expose himself to danger. Collins was the only fatality to occur during the ambush:

'If he had lived longer he might have become a great Irish Prime Minister. He was just thirty-two years old and had shown that he was capable of modifying his earlier views.'[3]

As it was, his death infuriated the pro-Treaty parties and the war dragged on. The IRA retrenched, falling back on a system of guerrilla warfare with flying columns and a series of assassinations that took out well-known figures along with many ordinary men, women and children.

The burning of landowners' houses, retaliation killings, torture and abuse all became part of the final stage of the civil war. It might not have been due totally to the death of Michael Collins, but his assassination certainly played a part.

Field Marshal Sir Henry Wilson, London (assassinated 22 June 1922)

Just two months before the assassination of Michael Collins, political killing had come to the streets of London. Field Marshal Sir Henry Wilkson, a First World War hero, recently elected as an Ulster MP, was shot and killed as he was entering his house on Eaton Place.

Wilson had just unveiled a war memorial on Liverpool Street Station and was therefore in full dress uniform. That made him an easy target.

Henry Wilson and his family had long been involved in Ulster politics, and Sir Henry himself was popularly supposed to have been one of the men behind the creation of the B Specials (the Ulster Special Constabulary, a quasi-military reserve police force). He certainly advocated a more military and violent approach by the police of Northern Ireland, and was a determined and passionate advocate for an independent Ulster.

Always more of a staff officer and advisor than battlefield soldier, and despite poor relations with General Haig, Wilson finished the Great War as Chief of the Imperial General Staff. It was a post he resigned in order to become an MP.

On 22 June 1922, Wilson was opening his front door when a bullet smashed into the wooden frame alongside him. He spun around, reaching for the ceremonial sword at his hip but only turning into the path of six more bullets. All hit him, two in the chest, and although his wife and servants managed to get him indoors, he died within minutes.

Two Irish assassins, supposedly working on the orders of Michael Collins, had carried out the assassination. They had been hand-picked for the job.

Reginald Dunne was commander-in-chief of the London Battalion of the IRA, and Joseph O'Sullivan had travelled from Ireland to carry out the killing. Both men had served in the British Amy during the recent war, O'Sullivan having lost a leg in the conflict.

As Wilson staggered and fell to the ground, Dunne and O'Sullivan fled, but the latter was handicapped by his wooden leg and was soon surrounded by angry members of the public. A lynching was clearly on the cards.

Dunne turned back to help his comrade, but both men were overpowered, beaten, battered and made prisoner. Two policemen and a member of the public were shot during the scuffle.

Dunne and O'Sullivan were hanged on10 August that year. The killing of Sir Henry Wilson brought the Irish troubles home to the British public. Not since the Phoenix Park murders of 1882, when Lord Frederick Cavendish and Thomas Burke were stabbed in Dublin's Phoenix Park, had the assassination of public figures caused such a furore.

The assassination of Field Marshal Wilson hardened public opinion, both in England and Ulster, against Irish Republican feelings and forces. And Collins, if he did order the assassination, did not have time or chance to enjoy his success.

The St Valentine's Day Massacre, Chicago (multiple assassinations, 14 February 1929)

By the end of the 1920s, assassination as an instrument of justice and retaliation had moved on beyond mere politics. It had become a weapon to be used by all elements of society, particularly the disreputable and self-interested. Nowhere is this better seen than in Chicago's infamous St Valentine's Day Massacre.

On the morning of 14 February 1929, seven gangsters, members of George 'Bugs' Moran's North Side Gang, gathered at a Lincoln Park garage in Chicago. They were waiting for the arrival of 'Bugs' Moran himself.

Prohibition, the US government ruling which outlawed public sales of alcohol, along with its production and transportation, had been introduced in 1920. The motives behind the passing and implementation of the law were sensible enough. However, Prohibition had done little more than create a gangster culture based around bootlegging, the illegal transportation and merchandizing of alcohol.

In Chicago, two rival underworld groups, 'Bugs' Moran's North Side Gang and Al Capone's largely Italian-influenced organization, were now facing each other, head-to-head, over control of the bootlegging industry.

On that cold February morning, disputes over territory and control of lucrative outlets such as the bootlegging establishments and illicit saloons were about to explode into violence and what quickly became open warfare.

Just after 10.30 am, a police car screeched to a halt outside of the garage. Four men, seemingly two policemen and two civilians, got out. They stormed into the garage, lined Moran's men against a wall and, using sub-machine guns and shotguns, mowed them down. It was the assassination of an enemy gang, pure and simple.

Only one man, Frank Gusenberg, survived the initial shooting. Despite intense questioning, he stuck to the gangster rule of not talking to the police, refusing to name any of the assassins. He died three hours later in hospital.

The killers exited the garage, the civilians in front of the two 'police officers', holding their hands in the air like captives. Nobody ever identified the assassins, speculation ranging from the Capone-controlled Egan's Rats to police seeking revenge for the killing of an officer's son.

Al Capone himself had a watertight alibi, being at his house in Florida. 'Bugs' Moran never showed at the garage, having spotted the police car before he made his entrance and hightailing it the other way. He spent the next hour in a coffee shop just down the street from the garage.

The seven victims included Albert Kachellek (AKA James Clark), who was Moran's brother-in-law and second-in-command. Other significant victims included the brothers and underworld enforcers Frank and Peter Gusenberg.

The St Valentine's Day assassinations caused a public outcry in Chicago. According to the press and public opinion, it was felt the city was not somewhere it was safe for honest citizens to live. It was a slight exaggeration but it was a warning that was taken seriously.

Prohibition, nine years since being introduced, was clearly having a negative effect. The ruling and ban on the making and sale of alcohol was duly abolished in 1933. By then, of course, the gangsters of men like Capone and Moran were well established as a significant part of the American underbelly.

The St Valentine's Day Massacre and other gangster-related incidents were not the only causes of the abolition of Prohibition, but they certainly played a significant role in its demise.

Chapter Five

A Low, Dishonest Decade, 1930–1939

The poet W.H. Auden once described the 1930s as 'a low, dishonest decade'. He might have added the word 'dishonourable', but in general Auden was right in his description.

The ten years in question saw the rise of Fascism, in particular Hitler's Nazi Party in Germany; it saw strikes, union walkouts and the effects of the Great Depression in all industrial-based countries. As emotion and frustration boiled over, it also saw a number of highly significant assassinations.

The First World War had been fought as 'the war to end all wars', but it clearly had not achieved anything of the kind. The Treaty of Versailles, by allocating all blame for the war onto Germany, did nothing more than ensure future conflict of some sort. It was just a matter of when it would happen. Once Hitler came to power, the timing was no longer in doubt.

Slowly but significantly, it became increasingly obvious that another war was coming, probably before the end of the decade. The period was marked by ten years of social deprivation and unhappiness, ten years of trumpeting and warmongering from Germany, Italy and Japan. It was a flexing of muscles that was matched by ignorance and lack of understanding in the appeasement-dominated countries of the world.

Germany, economically ruined by the Treaty of Versailles and the ravages of power-hungry, financially groping nations, turned eagerly to a man who promised relief and retribution from the squalor that had descended over most of Europe – Adolf Hitler. The fact that he did not – indeed could not – explain exactly how he would achieve this economic miracle hardly mattered.

When Hitler was asked to assume power – being invited to become Chancellor, not seizing the position, as many people still believe – the low decade reached a new low. Promises backed by violence were enough for a nation desperate for relief; initially at least, Hitler's regime prospered. Whether or not it would last was another matter altogether.

It was a time of gangster politics, a time of the gun rather than debate and discussion. And perhaps inevitably, it all began in Germany.

Ernst Rohm and the End of the SA, Germany (multiple assassinations, 1 July 1934)

During the 1920s, Adolf Hitler's Nazi Party was, in the main, a group of brawling thugs who, quite literally, beat their way to a position of dominance in the Bavaria region of the Weimar Republic. By the early 1930s, they controlled the streets, having decimated communist and socialist opponents in pitched battles on street corners and in the beer halls of cities like Munich.

The Sturmabteilung, or SA as they were almost universally known, made up the paramilitary wing of the Nazi Party. Regimentally clad in identical brown uniforms – designed and produced by the young, ambitious Nazi Party member, Hugo Boss – the SA were organized on a military basis, armed with weapons provided for them by their leader, Ernst Rohm.

Known as 'the machine gun King of Bavaria' because of his ability to illegally procure weapons from German Army stores, Rohm had spent several years in self-imposed exile in South America. However, he returned to Munich at the request of his friend Hitler to mould the street-corner enforcers of the embryonic Nazi Party into a private army.

A private army was what Hitler had wanted, and it was exactly what he got. By 1931, the SA consisted of over a million men, bitter and resentful, most of them out of work, feeling betrayed by the Weimar Republic. Ever more stringently, always a revolutionary at heart, Rohm was beginning to insist that the SA, his creation, could and should replace the Wehrmacht as Germany's main military force.

He believed, accurately enough, that all revolutions required a second uprising. Germany was no different from France or England, which had gone through the rigours of double revolutions centuries before. If the coming of Hitler was Germany's first revolution, could the coming of Ernst Rohm be the second?

By the early 1930s, with the SA controlling the streets and beginning to implement early anti-Semitic doctrines, mob violence and brutality were commonplace in Germany. In 1932 alone, there were more than 400 'battles' across the country, resulting in no fewer than eighty-two deaths – communists, socialists, Nazis and innocent bystanders alike.[1]

Rohm, egotistical and vain, was clear that he was exactly the person to implement a second revolution that would end the chaos. He had the means, the dedication and the backing to achieve it. Adored and venerated by his men, their loyalty to him was now outstripping even their love for Hitler. It was a dangerous situation.

The mood in the Nazi camp was ripe for action. After the initial outpouring of joy, the coming to power of the Nazis in 1933 had left many of Rohm's storm troopers unhappy. They were adamant that they had been left out in the division of the victory spoils. Hitler, Himmler, Goring and the rest were well catered for, revelling in their new status; the rank and file SA were out in the cold.

The storm troopers of the SA, the men who had been so important in Hitler's rise to power, wanted all of the things they had been promised – or believed they had been promised. They wanted back pay, they wanted positions of prestige and control, they wanted status. And one million unhappy brawlers was not an easy load to carry, either for Hitler or the SA leader. By the beginning of 1934, pressure on Ernst Rohm and Adolf Hitler was at a significant level.

That pressure came from two directions – from their own men and from the Wehrmacht. Despite the terms of the Treaty of Versailles, which severely limited its size, the army had always been and continued to be the basis of nearly all German politics and social standings. Now, the military arm of the nation, along with many of the wealthy businessmen who bankrolled the Nazis, saw Rohm's ambitions as a threat to their status, even their existence.

In the months after January 1933, following President Hindenburg's decision to appoint Adolf Hitler to the position of Chancellor, the Wehrmacht began to apply significant influence on Hitler and his top brass. Their message was simple: we like what you are doing, we will support you, but there is a price for our help.

The army's message and their price was straightforward enough – get rid of the SA before something unpleasant occurs; act before we are obliged to take up arms against you:

'In England, Russia and France one element was consistent: the need to eliminate people who had done their job and were now unable to see that they were redundant or out of time. In Germany in 1934 the brutal excision of the men who had helped Hitler to power, men who were suddenly dispensable elements in the wider game, played a vital role in securing the Nazi dictatorship.'[2]

To Hitler, anxious now to convert his position as Chancellor of a supposedly democratic nation into one of right-wing dictatorship, it was a risk worth taking. And yet, for several weeks, he could not bring himself to make that fatal decision to destroy the SA.

However, with Goring and Himmler acting as middle men and promising a solution in the near future, the army was, for the moment at least, pacified. Only their High Command remained expectant; preening themselves, they sat back to see what would happen.

They and the Nazis knew that the uneasy peace could not last long. President Hindenburg now became the third element of pressure, this time directed solely at Hitler. The aged president, despite increasing infirmity, confirmed the army view, informing Hitler that if he did not deal with the SA and sort out the violence in the streets, he would be forced to declare martial law and turn over control of the state to the army.

Despite the threat, yet again Hitler hesitated, unsure and reluctant to take what might be a fatal step. The men below him had no such reservations; as far as they were concerned, it was time to rid Germany and themselves of a potential opponent and his private army

In the early summer of 1934, Goring and Himmler, Hitler's two chief henchmen, along with a new addition to the cohort, Reinhard Heydrich, drew up a list of the men who would have to be eliminated. Top of the list, naturally, was Ernst Rohm. As if the assassination of Rohm needed justification, the rumour was now spread that in line with his desire for a second revolution, Rohm had been planning a coup.

It was all lies, the product of the fertile brains of Goring, Himmler and Heydrich, but it was effective. Forged letters and documents in Rohm's name, many of them with his signature at the bottom, supposedly to and from intelligence agencies in France, were put in front of the Chancellor. Everything was in place. All that was now needed was Hitler's formal approval.

Hitler had always been unsure. After all, Ernst Rohm was the only friend he had and the SA had been so valuable in his rise to power. Always a prevaricator, he took some persuading, but finally, early on 30 June 1934, he made his decision. What became known as the 'Night of the Long Knives' would be put into operation as Hitler struck with ruthless barbarity.

The chief implement behind the barbarity was the newly formed Schutzstaffel, the SS. Initially meant as Hitler's personal bodyguard, a role they filled to the end, they were also soon employed as a ruthless secret police who swore allegiance to the Fuhrer and of course to their chief, Heinrich Himmler. Their black uniforms, gleefully designed by Nazi Party member Hugo Boss, spread terror into the hearts of all German citizens, and in particular members of the SA. The SA were just thugs; the SS were evil murderers and assassins.

Rohm had played into the hands of his opponents in the Nazi Party by declaring a formal holiday for all members of the SA in the first week of July. Many of the senior officers joined Rohm at the Hotel Hanselbauer in the lakeside town of Bad Wiesee, south of Munich.

At dawn on 1 July 1934, SS hit squads, Hitler amongst them, smashed their way into the hotel bedrooms. Hitler himself arrested Rohm at gunpoint, screaming at him that he was a traitor. Rohm, half-asleep and confused, responded meekly with 'Heil Mein Fuhrer'.

Several of the SA officers, practicing homosexuals, were found in bed with their male partners. Hitler, who had previously ignored the practice, now seized on it as a further excuse for his actions, declaring it to be unnatural and obscene.

Arrests were followed by executions, dozens falling before the firing squads. Rohm spent the day in a prison cell before Theodor Eicke, commandant of Dachau Concentration Camp, and his deputy, Michael Lippert, appeared at his cell door. They were to be Rohm's final visitors:

> 'The Chancellor had tried his hardest to make Colonel [*sic*] Rohm shoot himself. He twice sent him a pistol which came back with the reply "If I am to be shot Hitler will have to do it himself."'[3]

Hitler did not shoot Rohm, but his two assassins did. Rohm faced his killers bare-chested and defiant. Eicke and Lippert shot him twice, at point-blank range.

Major Victims of The Night of the Long Knives, Germany (1 July 1934)

The exact number of victims assassinated during the Night of the Long Knives, as the excision of the SA soon became known, varies alarmingly. Some estimates put the figure as low as seventy or eighty – the German press said just ten. Other sources put the number of victims somewhere in the hundreds.

The exact number will probably never be known as the official lists compiled by Goring and his staff were extended by many 'unofficial' killings. Several thousand SA men were taken into custody, many of them ending up in concentration camps, where they lingered and, inevitably, many died.

Intended to be a cull of the SA, in particular Ernst Rohm and his closest comrades, Goring and Himmler took the opportunity of the Night of the Long Knives to dispose of other enemies of the state. It was done alongside settling a few personal grudges.

Analysis of the killings shows that in many cases the assassinations were acts of vengeance for past deeds or opposition to the Nazi Party. Number one on the list was Rohm, but there were many others who fell unsuspectingly to the guns of the assassins.

Gustav Ritter von Kahr was a previous Prime Minister of Bavaria who had the misfortune to be in office when Hitler had attempted a coup in 1923. Von Kahr was the driving force behind the quashing of the Beer Hall Putsch and then sending Hitler to prison, albeit for a very brief period. Now it was time for revenge.

On the evening of 30 June 1934, the 71-year-old retired politician was arrested by an SS commando at his apartment in Munich and taken to Dachau Concentration Camp. On the way there, he was badly beaten by members of the SS and upon arrival at the camp was sent to the detention building, known by the inmates as The Bunker. The following day he was shot.

The rumour quickly spread that his body, later found on Dachau Moor, had been hacked to pieces by pitchforks and bayonets. It was just a rumour, but one that enhanced the reputation and the sadism of the SS.

Karl Ernst was Berlin's Deputy Chief of Staff for the SA. As a former homosexual lover of Ernst Rohm, he was a significant figure in the organization. He and Rohm were still friendly, the SA leader having attended the wedding of Ernst only the day before the assassinations. Ernst and his new wife were en route to Bremerhaven to board a ship for their honeymoon when a car full of SS officers and officials overtook them and forced their vehicle off the road.

The SS men opened fire, wounding Ernst's wife and driver. Ernst was arrested and flown to Berlin for interrogation. His wife and driver were left to die or survive at the roadside. Both of them survived.

After a brief stay in Berlin, Karl Ernst was taken to the Lichterfelde Barracks. There, the same day, he was put in front of a firing squad and shot. Believing he was the victim of a plot by his former lover, Ernst died standing erect and shouting 'Heil Hitler'.

General Kurt von Schleicher, former Chancellor of Germany, was a man schooled in the art of intrigue and deception. Chancellor in the months before Hitler, he held the record for the shortest period in power, just fifty-seven days, and was desperate to regain his position.

He had been scheming for some time to split the Nazi Party and had hatched a plan to replace Hitler with Gregor Strasser, a long-time Nazi supporter who had now fallen out with Hitler. The plot went nowhere, but clearly von Schleicher was too dangerous to remain at large.

More recently, he had also been involved in talks with Rohm. The subject of their conversation has never been disclosed, but the fact that von Schleicher and Rohm had met was enough to guarantee their demise. Both men became early victims of Nazi paranoia.

Early on the morning of 30 June, an unsuspecting von Schleicher was at home in his villa on the outskirts of Berlin when the doorbell rang. The general answered the summons and was immediately shot down by a group of SS men dressed in civilian clothes. Von Schleicher's wife, Elisabeth, rushed to aid her husband and she too was instantly shot and killed.

General Kurt von Bredow, a close friend and associate of Schleicher, suffered a similar fate. A former head of the Abwehr, the intelligence unit of the army, he had been dismissed in the days before Hitler came to power. On the evening of 30 June, he was dining in a restaurant in the centre of Berlin. He finished his meal, left a substantial tip and headed for home:

'The waiter, a Gestapo informer, pocketed the tip and then phoned the police to say that their target was on the way; von Bredow was gunned down on his doorstep as soon as he reached his house.'[4]

Gregor Strasser was a former close colleague of Adolf Hitler and, along with his brother Otto, something of an intellectual. He has been called the brains behind the Nazi movement. He made the mistake of telling Hitler about von Schleicher's attempt to get him on his side, and a bitter row exploded. Strasser resigned from the Party and headed off for a holiday in Italy. Despite his assertions that he had finished with politics, Joseph Goebbels called Strasser 'a dead man walking'.

Strasser led an uneasy existence, but nothing prepared him for what was about to occur. He was arrested by police at noon on 30 June, dragged to the Prinz Albrechtstrasse Prison, supposedly on the orders of Hermann Goring, and shot later the same day.

Gregor's brother Otto, clearly reading the writing on the wall, fled Germany and became a vitriolic critic of Nazi Germany. So vocal was he in his opprobrium that Goebbels denounced him as 'public enemy number one' and put a price of half-a-million dollars on his head. Nobody ever tried to claim it.

Mistakes and Misreadings in the Night of the Long Knives

As with any form of mass assassination, there was always a propensity for mistakes, and several were made by the SS and police during the Night of the Long Knives. The wife of Kurt von Schleicher was not intended to be a victim, but she was in the wrong place at the wrong time and had seen the assassins at work. There was, in the eyes of the murder squad, no alternative.

Sometimes it was the press that got things wrong. According to several German newspapers, one of the supposed dead was Wolf-Heinrich Graf von Helldorf, former head of the Berlin SA. In fact,

Helldorf was not a victim but one of the organizers of the purge. He lived on in Germany until 1944.

The deaths of some of the victims remain inexplicable. Whether they were a mistake or personal vengeance is hard to know.

Notable amongst these was a defrocked priest named Father Bernhard Stemplfe, who had been a fellow prisoner of Hitler when he had served time in jail following the failed Beer Hall Putsch of 1923. Stemplfe had actually assisted in the editing of Hitler's book, *Mein Kampf*, while they were in prison together.

Stemplfe's body was found in a forest outside Munich. His neck was broken and there were three bullets in his heart, but the reason for his assassination was never clear. Rumour said that he had 'inside information' about the death of Hitler's niece and lover Geli Raubal, but the veracity of this story has never been proved.

The owner and the head waiter of the Bratwurst-Gloeckle restaurant and tavern in Munich, a popular drinking hole for Nazis, were both shot dead during the purge. Again, the motive for this is unclear. Perhaps they had overheard something and knew too much? Or maybe someone was just trying to get rid of his heavy bar bill!

Perhaps the most renowned mistake was the assassination of Wilhelm Eduard Schmid. The musician and music critic for one of the major Munich newspapers was seized while playing the cello at his home in the city. His wife and children tried to protect him, protesting that he had nothing to do with politics, but Schmid was dragged away. Four days later, his body was returned to the family in a closed coffin, along with the statement that it should not be opened.

Schmid had been mistaken for a local SA thug of the same name who had already been arrested and shot by another SS team. Deputy Fuhrer Rudolf Hess, in an attempt to hush up the affair, visited the grieving widow and arranged for her to receive a regular pension from the government. It was small consolation for such a dreadful mistake.

Aftermath of the Night of the Long Knives

In the wake of the Night of the Long Knives, the Wehrmacht, having made its pact with the Devil, felt its position safe. The fact that the army had stood by and allowed two of its generals, von Schleicher and von Bredow, to be assassinated without charge or trial seemed to count for nothing. It was merely collateral damage.

Soldiers of Germany now swore an oath of loyalty, not to their country but to Adolf Hitler. It was another step on the road to worldwide war.

No protest from the army was matched by a similar lack of response from the Catholic and Lutheran churches of Germany. President Hindenburg, who had praised Hitler for his prompt action to prevent the imaginary coup of Ernst Rohm, died on 2 August 1934, after which Hitler quickly combined the roles of president and chancellor. Germany was now a dictatorship.

Ernst vom Rath, Paris (assassinated on 9 November 1938 – heralding Kristallnacht)

Four years after the Night of the Long Knives, Ernst vom Rath was shot and killed inside the German Embassy in Paris.

Vom Rath was a minor Nazi official of no great standing, with no reason to suspect himself a target for assassination. His death on 9 November 1938, while in itself a tragedy, was a fairly minor political event.

Minor event it might have been, but the assassination marked the beginning of the Holocaust which was soon to erupt across Europe. Vom Rath, therefore, remains famous for the effects of his assassination, not for the actual killing itself.

Ernst vom Rath came from German nobility but had been a member of the Nazi Party for some years. In 1933, he was enrolled in the SA but managed to avoid death during the Night of the Long Knives. He duly became a junior member of the German Diplomatic Service, taking up the position of Third Secretary at the German Embassy in Paris.

His assassin was a 17-year-old Polish Jew by the name of Herschel Grynszpan, who, amongst other claims, professed that he was making a protest at the deportation of his parents from Germany.

At that time, Grynszpan's mother and father were incarcerated in an internment camp on the Polish frontier, living in squalid conditions, waiting to be sent back to their country of birth. Despite everything, both of them managed to survive the coming war.

Grynszpan arrived at the German Embassy early on the morning of 9 November. He met with vom Rath, pulled out a revolver and shot him five times in the chest, spleen and stomach.

Vom Rath died that evening. Grynszpan later alleged that he had been the victim of a sexual assault by vom Rath, but the accusation was never investigated and was hushed up by the Nazis, who were intent on using the martyrdom of the young diplomat for more dramatic purposes. Vom Rath died at 9.30 pm, and two hours later the first of Germany's many synagogues burst into flames.

That simple piece of arson was the beginning of Kristallnacht, the Night of Broken Glass, which was, in turn, a forerunner of the Holocaust. From this one assassination and the immediate repercussions came open slaughter, and eventually the death of six million Jews.

Kristallnacht was a two-day pogrom, an orgy of unfettered hate and government-approved crime, with massive anti-Jewish violence whipped up by Joseph Goebbels. While not an accidental event, there was a degree of opportunism behind the violence.

The assassination of Ernst vom Rath gave the Nazis the opportunity for which they had been waiting. There had already been persecution of German Jews, in particular the closing or barring of shops and the dismissal of Jews from certain professions, but this was the chance to take a significant blow at the Jewish community. Kristallnacht was just the start of violent and unrestrained oppression.

Once it had begun, the violence was carefully controlled and organized. It became a mass killing that was put into operation in the twelve hours between the shooting that morning and vom Rath's death in the evening.

The SS, the remnants of the SA and members of the general public were marshalled into what were little more than 'destruction squads' that targeted synagogues, Jewish businesses and Jewish homes right across Germany.

In that brief space of time, Hitler also promoted the dying man to the rank of legal counsel, first class. A state funeral was held on 1 December, Foreign Minister Joachim von Ribbentrop declaring that the Nazi government was now dealing with nothing less than open warfare. 'The Jews have fired the first shot,' he proclaimed. 'We accept the challenge.'

During Kristallnacht, 267 synagogues across the length and breadth of Germany were burned down, along with countless Jewish businesses and houses. Most of the synagogues and businesses were looted before being destroyed.

At least ninety-one Jews were killed in the two-day orgy of violence on 9 and 10 November at the urging of the Nazi government. Some 30,000 arrests were also made.

There were never any charges or reasons for particular arrests or destruction of property. Beaten and abused, the Jewish victims were dragged from their homes and sent to concentration camps, where many of them died in the years ahead.

As for Herschel Grynszpan, he was never tried for the assassination of Ernst vom Rath but remained in the custody of the French. He was imprisoned by the French authorities after the shooting, but escaped during the French defeat of 1940.

He was rearrested, this time by the Nazis, and packed off to Sachsenhausen Concentration Camp, where he disappeared from view. It is more than likely that he was killed or died from starvation during the final stages of the war.

Chapter Six

The Second World War and its Immediate Aftermath

The Second World War broke out in the autumn of 1939 when Nazi troops, on the pretext of countering or avenging a Polish attack on a German radio station, drove deeply into the heartland of Poland. By 1942, the intrusion had escalated into a worldwide conflict that saw millions of individuals, both civilians and soldiers from across the globe, killed, maimed and displaced.

There were a number of assassinations during the war, by people from all spectrums of political affinity. Individuals like Winston Churchill, Roosevelt and Hitler were obvious targets, and plans for their assassinations were carefully considered by their opponents. None of these plans were ever put into operation, and the most significant of the attempts on a leader's life, the unsuccessful Bomb Plot of July 1944, was carried out by members of Hitler's own army, not by enemy agents.

By 1939, Russia, simmering under the dictatorship of Joseph Stalin, had already experienced several years of murder and mayhem as Communist Party leaders and old comrades were sacrificed to the guns of Stalin's hit squads. Leon Trotsky – real name Lev Davidovich Bronstein – was one of the lucky ones. He managed to escape Stalin's wrath, temporarily at least.

Leon Trotsky, Mexico City (assassinated 21 August 1940)

Viewed by many as the lynchpin of the Russian Revolution, Leon Trotsky was a Jewish Marxist who, before the 1917 Revolution, had spent much of his life in exile, both at home and abroad.

Originally a fairly moderate Menshevik, Trotsky moved on to hold a number of different positions in the Bolshevik regime, negotiating the Treaty of Brest-Litovsk which ended the war with Germany in March 1918. He also founded the Red Army, developing it from the small Red Guard, and then led it to victory in 1922 in the civil war against the White Russian supporters of the deposed Czar Nicholas II.

In the manoeuvring for position after Lenin's death, Joseph Stalin emerged as the eventual victor. His subsequent purges are well known, in particular the Great Terror when, over a two-year period, around 750,000 individuals were killed, a further 30,000 being sent to endure a slower, more lingering death in the gulag camps of Siberia.

Stalin was clear that anyone who had connections to Lenin's government or with the Bolshevik Party in general was a potential threat. Leon Trotsky was, in his opinion, the biggest threat of all.

Trotsky's belief in exporting the revolution and establishing worldwide communism was alien to everything Stalin stood for. Trotsky was duly expelled from the Politburo in 1926 and the Communist Party a year later. After a period of internal exile, he was exiled from Russia in 1929:

'He was received by the government of Turkey and settled on the island of Pinkipo where he worked on his autobiography and history of the Russian Revolution. After four years in Turkey, Trotsky lived in France and Norway before he was granted asylum in Mexico.'[1]

Much to the fury of the Russian leader, Trotsky continued in all his writings to berate Stalin and his regime. In 1936, Stalin reciprocated by sentencing Trotsky to death, in absentia. This signalled the beginning of a long persecution, with many believing that Stalin's reign of terror would not be complete so long as Leon Trotsky was still alive.

Several attempts were made on Trotsky's life, notably a May 1940 assault by a number of NKVD officers who pumped more than 300 machine-gun bullets into the bedroom of his house in Mexico City.

Trotsky and his wife, lying prone on the bedroom floor, survived the attack. Three months later, he was not so lucky.

Ramon Mercader was the son of Spanish and Cuban parents, close friends of Trotsky. Mercader, an avowed communist in the pay of the NKVD, did not really know Trotsky all that well, but was formally introduced to him by an accomplice.

On Tuesday, 20 August 1940, he appeared at Trotsky's house on the pretext of showing him an article he was writing and inveigled the exiled Russian to his own studio, where they could read and discuss the document. Always short-sighted, Trotsky bent over the article, eyes on the print. Then Mercader struck. He had placed his coat on the table, an ice axe in the pocket, within easy grasp:

> 'I gave him a tremendous blow on the head. The man screamed in such a way that I will never forget as long as I live. His scream was very long, infinitely long, and it still seems to me as if that scream were piercing my brain.'[2]

The axe had pierced Trotsky's skull, driving nearly 3 inches into his brain. Despite the pain, he turned on Mercader and wrestled him to the floor, preventing a second blow and breaking the assassin's hand. Trotsky's bodyguards, alerted by the noise, charged into the room and began to beat Mercader. There is little doubt that they would have beaten him to death, but Trotsky stopped them, saying that the man needed to be questioned.

Taken to hospital, Trotsky survived for twenty-four hours before dying on 21 August. He was 60 years old. Mercader was arrested by the Mexican police, convicted of the murder and sentenced to twenty years in prison. He served his full sentence, being released in 1960. He then changed his name, travelled the world and eventually settled in Cuba, where he died in the late 1970s.

From a political viewpoint, Trotsky's death had little or no effect. It was simply another example of Stalin's capacity for revenge, the long arm of Soviet 'justice'.

Reinhard Heydrich, Prague (assassinated 4 June 1942)

Adolf Hitler once referred to Reinhard Heydrich as 'the man with an iron heart'. Coming from Hitler, that was meant as a complement. It is a remark with which most people would agree. He was certainly one of the 'darkest' of all Nazi officials, responsible for countless deaths in Eastern Europe and commonly known, by friend and foe, as 'the hangman'.

Cashiered from the German Navy for conduct unbecoming of an officer and gentleman by proposing to two women at the same time, Heydrich joined the Nazi Party the day after his discharge papers were received. Six weeks later, on 14 July 1931, he was enrolled into the SS. His progress up the ranks was rapid.

Shortly after he joined the SS, he met with Heinrich Himmler and impressed him with plans for a counter-intelligence service. On 1 August 1931, he was made chief of the new spy unit and by October had created a wide network of spies and informers. As a reward, Himmler had him promoted to the rank of Sturmbannfuhrer, the equivalent of major in the British Army.

Despite rumours of a Jewish background, a story spread by jealous opponents, Heydrich continued to thrive, making sure that the accusations were dispelled. By April 1934 he was head of the Gestapo, had assisted Himmler and Goring in the destruction of Ernst Rohm and was clearly being marked down as a successor to Himmler.

When German police forces were consolidated under Himmler in 1936, Heydrich was appointed his deputy. Now there were no more allegations about his background, and even Himmler grew wary of the one senior Nazi who looked like Hitler's perfect Aryan.

When war broke out in 1939, Heydrich, eager to play a full part in the conflict, flew combat missions until Hitler and Himmler grounded him, forbidding him to put his life in danger. He became Reich Protector of Bohemia and Moravia in 1941, sealing his fist over the position by declaring: 'We will Germanise the Czech vermin.'[3]

His influence spread, organizing the Einsatzgruppen killing squads that operated in the wake of the army during the invasion of Russia. Thousands of Russian soldiers and civilians from the conquered countries were killed thanks to Heydrich's 'efficiency'.

One of his first tasks had been to implement the Night and Fog Decree, overseeing the disappearance of approximately 7,000 Czech nationals who were deemed to be a danger to the Third Reich.

In Prague, Heydrich set about destroying Czech culture. In January 1942, as Chief of Reich Security, he chaired the infamous Wannsee Conference that finalized plans for what became known as the Final Solution. For the Czech government in exile, there was only one thing to do – Heydrich would have to be assassinated.

Trained by Winston Churchill's Special Operations Executive, two Czech soldiers were eventually chosen to carry out Operation Anthropoid, as the assassination attempt was known. They were Jan Kubis and Joseph Gabcik, both willing to sacrifice their lives if necessary. On 15 April 1942, they were parachuted into Czechoslovakia and, without any means of contacting England, seemed to disappear from view. Isolated and alone, the two men prepared their plans. Ideas were brought up and then discounted. Finally, they hit on the right one.

Heydrich, with supreme arrogance and disdain for Czech opposition, always took the same route to his headquarters every morning. He travelled in an open-topped car, the vehicle having to slow down to a crawl in order to negotiate a corner at the bottom of a steep hill. That was where, on 27 May, the two assassins were waiting.

As the Mercedes slowed to a virtual halt at the bottom of the hill, Gabcik stepped out in front of it, aimed his Sten gun and pressed the trigger. Nothing happened; the gun had jammed. Rather than cower for cover, Heydrich leapt to his feet, intending to fire his pistol. Before he could do this, Kubis threw a hand grenade which exploded under the car, driving bits of the seat and other material up into Heydrich's body.

The assassins fled, Heydrich and his driver in pursuit until the Reich Protector collapsed, finally able to go no further. Taken to hospital, it was clear that his injuries were serious. There was damage to his spleen, one of his lungs had collapsed and a rib was shattered.

However, despite running a high fever, Heydrich appeared to be recovering. Then, a week later, despite the attention of Himmler's personal physician, who had been flown in to treat him, Heydrich collapsed and died, probably from septicaemia.

Hitler was furious; Himmler perhaps less so. Heydrich was a clear threat to him. Himmler had created a monster in Heydrich, one that was bound to haunt him at some stage, and it has been suggested that his doctor might have had a hand in the death, although nothing has ever been proved.

Immediate reprisals were ordered. The villages of Lidice and Lezaky, supposedly because of connections – false connections, as it turned out – to the Czech underground, were destroyed. The inhabitants of the villages were shot or packed off to concentration camps, where their fate was just the same. Estimates vary but, including relatives of the assassins and citizens plucked off the streets of Prague, somewhere in the region of 1,300 Czechs were killed.

The two assassins eluded the SS and the German Army for three weeks. They, along with other Czech partisans, hid in the crypt of the Cathedral of Saints Cyril and Methodius in Prague, but were betrayed by a colleague named Karel Curda. A huge reward of a million marks had been too great a temptation for him. He did not have time to enjoy his sudden wealth, however. Imprisoned and convicted of treachery, in the post-war years he was hanged in Prague.

A force of 750 well-armed SS men now besieged the cathedral. Furious defence by the assassins kept them at a distance for some time, and in desperation, the Prague Fire Brigade was ordered to pump water into the crypt. With ammunition running out, Gabcik, Kubis and the partisans were either shot or committed suicide rather than fall into German hands.

Heydrich might have gone, but Karl Frank, who took over his duties, was almost as ruthless. There remains the niggling question

– was the assassination of Reinhard Heydrich, evil as he might have been, worth the lives of so many innocent Czech men, women and children? Apart from the Holocaust, of which Heydrich was one of the principal architects, the assassination led to the worst atrocity of the war. Interestingly, there were no further attempts to assassinate high-ranking German or British officers and individuals during the Second World War. Perhaps that answers the question.

Admiral Isoroku Yamamoto, Bougainville, Solomon Islands (assassinated 18 April 1943)

'I fear we have awakened a sleeping giant and filled him with a terrible resolve' – whether or not Admiral Yamamoto ever uttered those famous words after the Japanese attack on Pearl Harbor in December 1941, the phrase was certainly pertinent.

A Japanese attack on the USA while the two countries were still at peace was a game of chance, and with the US carriers away from Pearl Harbor, it was one that ultimately failed. It did, however, give rise to another well-known utterance, and this time there was no doubt about its origin and veracity. As President Franklin Delano Roosevelt said, '7th December 1941 will go down in history as a date of infamy.'

Yamamoto, who had spent two periods as Naval Attache in Washington and knew the country and the American people well, did not want war with the USA. He knew the chances of victory were slim. If the Japanese were to achieve anything like success, it had to be done within the first eighteen months of war. After that, the balance of power would swing inexorably back to the Americans.

Yamamoto had spent most of his life in the Imperial Japanese Navy, losing two fingers at the Battle of Tsushima in 1905 when the Russian fleet was destroyed in thirty minutes, rising to the position of commander-in-chief at the start of the Second World War. It was a distinguished career.

Archduke Franz Ferdinand.

The ripped and bloodstained
uniform of Franz Ferdinand.

Czar Nicholas II and his son Alexi, reduced to chopping wood during their imprisonment.

Czar Nicholas and his family.

Exotic, erotic and dramatic but a terrible spy, Mata Hari.

Pancho Villa, Mexican revolutionary and bandit chief.

Happier days for SA chief Ernst Rohm, shown here with Hitler and fellow Nazi leaders.

Trotsky's house, where he lived out his final years.

Leon Trotsky with his second wife, 1932.

Pat Garrett, the killer of Billy the Kid.

Reinhard Heydrich, (left) according to Hitler, the man with 'an iron heart.'

Election poster for President McKinley.

Newspaper headline about the assassination of Michael Collins.

Japanese Admiral Yamamoto, architect of the Japanese attack on Pearl Harbor in 1941.

Mahatma Gandhi.

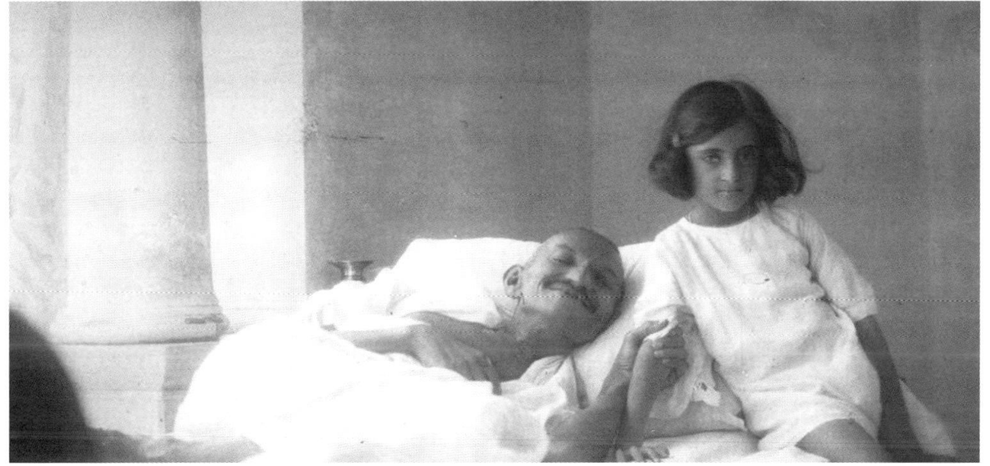

Peaceful, non violent protest was the hallmark of Gandhi's aims and ambitions.

The dead body of Mussolini (second from left), hanging from a garage forecourt, alongside his mistress.

African civil rights leader Steve Biko.

Members of the first independent Congolese government.

Fidel Castro, subject to many assassination plots, shown here with Che and other supporters.

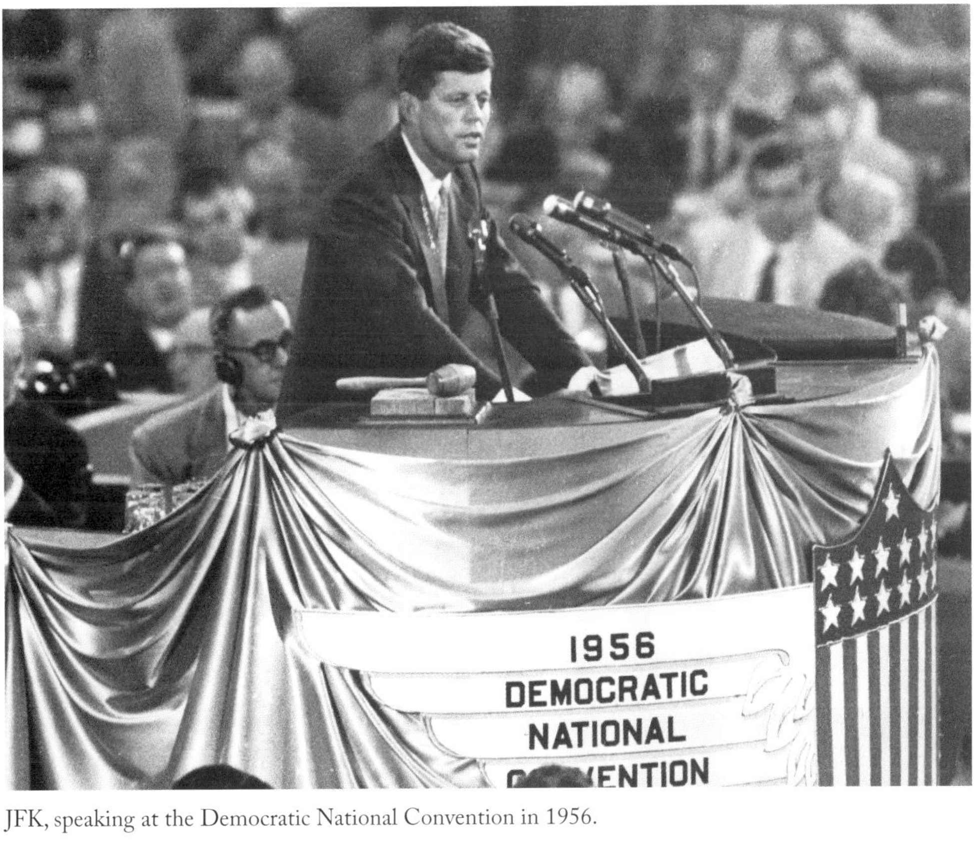

JFK, speaking at the Democratic National Convention in 1956.

Malcolm X poses with a gun. The threat to his life was real.

Louis Mountbatten, IRA victim.

Sharon Tate, murdered or assassinated.

John Lennon,
remembered outside
the Cavern Club.

John and Yoko Ono, one a victim, the other a witness.

Martin Luther King, the most significant human rights advocate of the 20th century.

Pablo Escobar, gangster, politician and drug cartel leader.

Ronald Reagan, US President, lucky to survive an assassination attempt.

President Sadat of
Egypt watching
a parade.

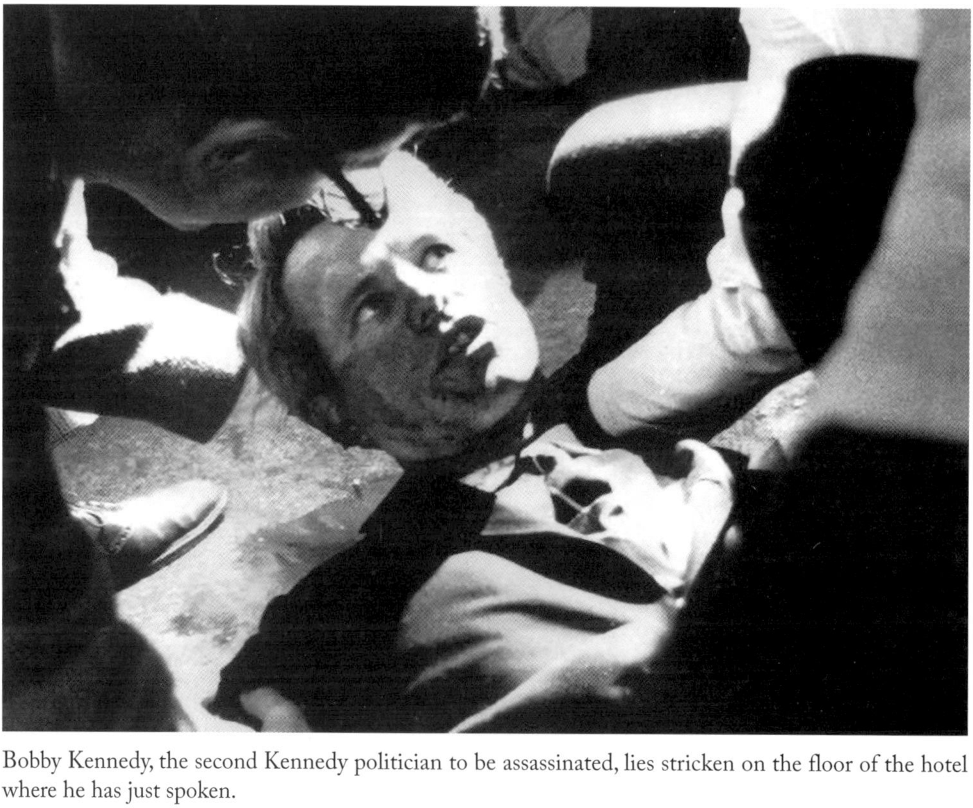

Bobby Kennedy, the second Kennedy politician to be assassinated, lies stricken on the floor of the hotel
where he has just spoken.

Despite his popularity within the navy, Yamamoto was operating in what was clearly a right-wing, reactionary Japan. His outspoken views put him in direct opposition to the warlike and bellicose politicians and army commanders of Japan. There was a very real possibility that he might even be assassinated by some army or civilian hothead. Going back to sea as commander of the Imperial fleets was considered the best way to keep him alive.

In the wake of Pearl Harbor, Japanese successes began to pile up one after the other as their military machine took the Imperial flag into the Philippines, Malaya, Burma and even to the border of India. Soon, however, as Yamamoto had predicted, the tide of war turned against the Japanese. As recently conquered territories returned once more to Allied hands, Japanese morale plummeted and, following the loss of Guadalcanal, in an effort to boost that morale once again, Yamamoto undertook an inspection tour of Japanese territories in the South Pacific.

Unfortunately for Yamamoto, US Naval Intelligence intercepted and decoded a message giving all of the Japanese admiral's destinations. More importantly, Yamamoto's times of arrival and departure at each location were also known to the Americans. Yamamoto, it was decided, needed to be 'taken out', removed from the equation.

It is not clear if President Roosevelt ordered or approved of what was effectively an assassination, but the naval command under Chester Nimitz certainly did. Yamamoto, considered the architect of the Pearl Harbor attack, was as unpopular in the USA as he was in the Japanese Army. There was a real desire for revenge, the mission to kill Yamamoto being christened Operation Vengeance.

The decision to assassinate him was something of a foregone conclusion, but it was still controversial, the Geneva Convention having prohibited cold-blooded personal attacks on senior enemy officers. However, in the view of Nimitz and other members of the naval command, this would be an act of war rather than an assassination.

On 18 April 1943, Yamamoto was due to fly to an island in the Solomons. A squadron of P38 Lockhead Lightnings, the only US aircraft with sufficient range to intercept the two bomber aircraft that made up the Japanese force, was assembled. Flying at treetop height, the Americans made the journey in two hours; the two units, American Lightnings and Japanese Mitsubishis, met over the island of Bougainville.

In the ensuing dogfight, Lieutenant Rex Barber attacked the first Japanese bomber, which happened to be the aircraft carrying Yamamoto. Barber kept firing until smoke was seen to pour out of the Mitsubishi's left engine. A second Lightning, piloted by Tom Lamphier, also began to fire at the Japanese bomber, and within a few minutes Yamamoto's plane went into a steep dive, crashing into the jungle on Bougainville.

Yamamoto's body was found the next day, still sitting upright in his seat, which had been thrown clear of the aircraft. He had two bullet wounds, one to the left shoulder, the other to the left side of the jaw. The second bullet had exited above the right eye and would have been a fatal wound. Credit for the 'kill' was shared between Barber and Lamphier.

News of Yamamoto's death was kept secret from the Japanese people for over a month, although his body was quickly cremated in Papua New Guinea. He was given a state funeral back in Japan on 5 June 1943. Already demoralised, news of the admiral's assassination hit hard at the Japanese belief in the war effort. As far as Nimitz and the others were concerned, that further drop in enemy morale justified the assassination.

Benito Mussolini, northern Italy (assassinated 28 April 1945)

Benito Mussolini, Fascist dictator of Italy and forerunner in a wave of right-wing politicians to achieve power and status during the twentieth century, survived numerous assassination attempts during his lengthy career. He finally fell foul of communist partisans when he was out of office and attempting to flee the country. Some might say it was poetic justice.

A newspaper journalist by profession, Mussolini was also a socialist, at least to begin with. He advocated military involvement in the First World War, a stance which saw him expelled from the Italian Socialist Party. He fought in the Royal Italian Army until he was wounded and discharged in 1917. Following this experience, his viewpoint changed and he became rabidly nationalistic in his politics.

By 1922, he was leader of the Italian Fascist Party, and on 28 October led nearly 30,000 blackshirts – so called because of their distinctive black uniforms – in the infamous 'March on Rome'. There was no actual march, but with Fascists arriving from all directions to gather in the Italian capital, Mussolini, always ready to exploit any publicity angle, declared that the march had been completed.

Demanding the resignation of the Italian Prime Minister and the appointment of a right-wing government, the Fascists reflected opinion of much of the country. King Victor Emmanuel III bowed to their demands and appointed Mussolini to the post of prime minister. Il Duce, as he soon became known, quickly got to work. He immediately founded a force of secret police to remove opposition, outlawed worker strikes and established a 'party dictatorship' in Italy.

Mussolini's leadership was based on the cult of personality, but his never had a great deal of substance or depth about it. Even his much-quoted achievement – 'At least he made the trains run on time' – was a lie, as the improvement in the Italian railways had begun long before he came to power.

Despite an innate weakness at the heart of his organization, over his twenty years in power Mussolini developed his Fascist supporters and the young men of Italy from a shapeless mass into a jackboot-stomping, goose-stepping force of what appeared to be power and belief in their leader. The straight-arm salute, the ranting speeches, the marching songs and the unified bellowing responses were a model for Hitler and his Nazis, but closer examination revealed that Mussolini's war machine was all show and little substance.

'Living space' became a creed for Mussolini's Fascists, and over subsequent years they conquered Ethiopia and made Albania an Italian protectorate, before conquering the country in 1939. Mussolini moved on to annex the city of Fiume in northern Yugoslavia.

As leader of Fascist Italy, Mussolini withdrew his country from the League of Nations and formed an alliance with Germany and Japan. Like Hitler, he sent his air force and ground troops to assist Franco in the Spanish Civil War. He was wary of Germany's strength, however, despatching troops to guard the Brenner Pass in the Alps in an attempt to halt Germany's rapid military progress.

Despite his alliance with Germany, when war erupted in 1939, Mussolini initially kept Italy as a non-belligerent nation. That lasted until the success of the Germans in France in 1940, when Mussolini, eager not to miss out on the spoils of victory, joined the conflict on Germany's side. It was undoubtedly the biggest mistake of his life.

What followed was disaster after disaster, with Hitler being forced to send troops to help shore up failing Italian operations in Greece and North Africa.

With the Allied conquest of Sicily in 1943, Mussolini found himself facing a vote of no confidence from the Italian people. Food and fuel shortages, enemy bombing raids and defeat of their armies had destroyed whatever adulation remained for Mussolini. It was a far cry from the heady 1930s, when he was seen a figure of respect and even people like Winston Churchill held him up as a man of principle and logic.

Dismissed by Victor Emanuel III, Mussolini was taken into custody by the Italian Carabinieri in the summer of 1943. On 12 September that year, he was rescued by a German commando unit from his imprisonment in an isolated mountain-top hotel. Taken to see Hitler, it was clear that Mussolini was now no more than a pawn, but he accepted his new position and the German-led posting as head of the Italian Social Republic. He spent the next eighteen months in a villa at Lake Garda, preening and posing but all the time knowing that his days in the sunlight were over:

'Seven years ago I was an interesting person. Now I am little more than a corpse … My star has fallen. I have no fight left in me.'[4]

Meanwhile, the new Italian government pulled out of the war but found their country occupied by German forces and by invading Allies. They subsequently declared war on Germany, a meaningless but annoying gesture for Hitler.

On 25 April 1945, with Allied troops pouring into northern Italy, Mussolini's phantom republic crumbled. Realizing that there was now no other option, he and his mistress, Clara Petacci, set out for a place of security in Switzerland. Two days later, they were stopped alongside Lake Como by Italian communist partisans who had no love for Il Duce.

The escapees were held at gunpoint while the partisans consulted their headquarters, demanding to know what they should do with them. The answer was simple – Mussolini must die.

Mussolini, Petacci and several of their accompanying colleagues were summarily shot. Their bodies were unceremoniously thrown into the back of a van and taken to Milan, where they were dumped in the ancient piazza. The bodies were kicked and spat on by the public before being hung upside down by their heels from the roof of a petrol station in the city. Even then more indignities were heaped upon them, the bodies being regularly stoned for as long as they hung there.

Mussolini, like Rudolf Hess, later became something of a cult hero for neo-Fascists, who saw only the personality that Il Duce had tried to promote. His dream of establishing a new Italian Empire based around the Mediterranean basin never grew beyond an imaginary conjuring of impossible successes.

Benjamin 'Bugs' Siegel, Beverley Hills, California (assassinated 20 July 1947)

The USA was brought into the Second World War by the Japanese attack on Pearl Harbor in December 1941. Nevertheless, there were still many Americans who ignored their patriotic duty, taking the opportunity to exploit the situation and make themselves a small fortune. Gangsters were a classic example of this, and Benjamin 'Bugs or Bugsy' Siegel was one of the most successful.

A New York boy from a European Jewish background, Siegel was born in 1906. He developed his links with the gangster world at an early age, leaving school to join a gang on Lafayette Steet on the Lower East Side of Manhattan.

His involvement with serious crime began with the Jewish mob, alongside his friend Myer Lansky, using his violent streak – along with a charming personality – to get himself noticed. Armed robbery, protection rackets and murder were meat and drink to him. He was also heavily involved with New York's Italian-American Mafia and with the National Crime Syndicate, and became one of the founder members of Murder Inc.

In 1936, Siegel moved to California, where he became a hit man and a big noise in the bootlegging and protection rackets. He settled in Beverley Hills, alongside the movie stars of the era, and was soon on friendly terms with actors such as George Raft, Clark Gable and Jean Harlow. His wild and luxurious parties became the talk of the town.

He also travelled to Italy, where, thanks to the machinations of Countess Dorothy di Frasso, he met Mussolini and tried to sell him armaments. He met with Goring and Goebbels too, but was not impressed with the Nazis, whom he considered to be lacking in style.

It was perhaps inevitable that Siegel and the various mobs with which he was involved should cast envious eyes on the developing gambling resort of Las Vegas in Nevada. They part-financed several of the early casinos and Siegel became involved with the building of The Flamingo, one of the first massive hotels and entertainment centres in the town.

When William R. Williamson, the main investor in the hotel project, ran out of money, Bugsy Siegel took over on behalf of the mob. Opening night was, however, a disaster thanks to a massive rain storm and virtually nobody turned up. The hotel closed within a few weeks.

The Flamingo opened again in March 1947, but the mob now had serious doubts about the charming and erudite Bugsy Siegel. He had, they believed, creamed off a million dollars from the hotel and the project, perhaps with his girlfriend, perhaps alone. And nobody did that to the mob.

On 20 July 1947, as Bugsy sat comfortably in his Beverley Hills home, a sniper took aim and shot him repeatedly in the head and body. Firing through the window and from a distance, there was no real danger of the assassin being identified or caught and the murder, even now, remains unsolved. Siegel was hit by several bullets and died almost immediately.

Benjamin Bugsy Siegel had made a lot of money for the mob and for himself, but the cost was horrendous – assassination at the hands of an unknown sniper.

Mohandas Karamchand (Mahatma) Gandhi, Delhi (assassinated 30 January 1948)

Most people know the name Mahatma Gandhi, the Hindu scholar and independence activist who was opposed to violence but who finished up as a victim of the very violence he had spent his life trying to eliminate.

Born in 1869, at the high point of the British Raj, Gandhi became a lawyer and anti-colonialist, working in the rabidly racist cities and towns of South Africa before returning to his native India. There, he commenced his long-running programme of non-violent protest against the British Empire. His reputation was already huge, the name Mahatma, from the Sanskrit for 'Great Soul', having already been bestowed upon him by the people he was trying to help.

Leader of the Indian Nationalist Congress, Gandhi was more than a mere political force. He was the spiritual leader of India, a man whose obvious sincerity transcended party and religious beliefs. He could be ruthless, particularly to himself, but he was also caring and compassionate.

During the 1920s and 1930s, Gandhi worked hard at what soon became a national campaign for independence from Britain. Other aims included creating acceptance and friendship between India's two primary religions and expanding women's rights.

Dressed in a traditional short dhoti and usually going about barefoot, Gandhi lived a life of self-sufficient abstinence. Jailed many times, he made fasting a hugely effective political art, of particular significance in his campaign to create unity and harmony between Hindus and Muslims.

The Muslim desire for a separate homeland, an idea actively promoted by Muhammad Ali Jinnah, founder of the Muslim League and later the first leader of Pakistan, was contrary to everything Gandhi wanted or had ever dreamed about.

However, he reluctantly accepted the creation of a Muslim state as inevitable and agreed to work alongside men like Jinnah in an attempt to keep the peace. It was a forlorn hope. Violence between Hindu and Muslim people had been a regular occurrence for many years, but now there was a vicious depth of feeling from both sides of the religious divide.

After independence from Britain and the creation of Pakistan alongside India in 1947, Gandhi continued to speak and campaign for unity between the two religions and the newly created nations.

Violence between members of the religious sects erupted while the two divisions were still being established, and Gandhi undertook several fastings in an attempt to end the killings. He was partially effective, and the rioting and killing did at least reduce, but the fasting was physically and emotionally draining on an old man who had given so much. Nevertheless, it is estimated, that the massacres, particularly of refugees fleeing either from India to Pakistan or Pakistan to India, cost somewhere in the region of a million lives.

By January 1948, Mahatma Gandhi was in Delhi, where, despite his weakened state, he preached daily, attempting to shame the two communities into establishing some sort of peace. It was his life's work and nothing was going to stop him; nothing apart from death.

On the evening of 30 January, escorted and helped by his two nieces, he walked slowly to a pergola in the gardens of Birla House. The evening service at the pergola, invariably led by Gandhi, sometimes attracted as many as 800 or 900 supporters. On this occasion, over 500 members of the public were waiting. Among them was a fanatical newspaper editor by the name of Nathuram Vinayak Godse:

> 'Gandhi was shot dead at point blank range by a Hindu fanatic [Godse] … At his trial Godse accused Gandhi of being "unfairly favourable towards the Muslims" and said he had brought "rack and ruin and destruction to millions of Hindus".'[5]

Godse had been in favour of an undivided India, seeing Gandhi's acceptance and support of Pakistan as a betrayal. He, along with an accomplice named Narayan Apte, was hanged on 15 November 1948. Gandhi survived for just half an hour after the shooting. He did not recover consciousness, and there remains some dispute as to whether or not he uttered his famous alleged final words, 'Oh God', as two bullets hit home.

As far as the results of assassinations go, the killing of Mahatma Gandhi was perhaps the least successful of them all. Godse had hoped that the differences between Hindus and Muslims would be solved with Gandhi's death, but nothing could have been further from the truth. Antipathy still exists and the two countries have locked horns several times, particularly over the ownership of Kashmir.[6]

The assassination deprived India – and the world – of a great peacemaker and a truly remarkable human being.

Chapter Seven

The Troubled and Troublesome Sixties

If the twentieth century was the most brutal of all periods as far as the process of assassination was concerned, then the 1960s have to be regarded as standing at the height of the phenomenon. Presidents and politicians, aid workers and human rights activists – nobody was exempt, everyone was a potential target.

The Sixties was a time of liberation and freedom of expression. It was an age of free love, hippies and 'power to the people'. The benefits of such an approach, after the restrictions of the previous twenty years, were obvious. But there was also a downside – it was freedom for everybody, whether good, bad or indifferent. And some of the choices people made were nothing short of monstrous.

Possibly more worrying, several of the assassinations or attempted killings were organized and carried out by governments around the globe. Britain's MI6 and the CIA in America were at the forefront of this bizarre and dangerous move, albeit mostly with unsuccessful results, it has to be said.

Some of their efforts were ludicrous, many of them coming to nothing. The failures included things like the CIA's plan to provide tainted cigars that would make Fidel Castro's beard fall out and cause him to lose face with the Cuban people. The mistakes of MI5 and MI6 mostly centred on an inane belief that double agents like the Cambridge Five or renowned prison escaper George Blake were really genuine and honest guys who would never betray their country.

In the post-war period, anti-colonialism was rife, particularly in the Far East and Africa, which led to a wide range of assassination attempts, along with interventions by countries such as Great Britain, Belgium, France and the USA.

Patrice Lumumba, Kananga, Africa (assassinated 17 January 1961)

Highly intelligent, with a passion for poetry and the work of Enlightenment writers like Voltaire, Patrice Lumumba was a prime mover in the fight for Congolese independence. He was always something of a marked man, if not from rival groups in the Congo then certainly from the USA and Belgian intelligence agents who were prepared to consider a degree of independence for their colonial African state but at their pace, not that of the Congolese.

In 1960, Lumumba became Prime Minister of the Democratic Republic of Congo. His politics were moving slowly but significantly towards those of the USSR and China, the two major communist powers in the world. They were states where he could be sure of support for creating a totally independent Congo. It was, however, a swing that the USA, paranoid as ever where the advance of 'the left' was concerned, could not allow.

Lumumba became a target for CIA intervention, the plot apparently approved by President Eisenhower. It was a highly imaginative idea – perhaps ridiculous might be a better description – that involved spreading a toxic substance on his toothbrush and thus poisoning him to death. The plan was called off when CIA agents in the Congo saw no possible way of carrying it out.

The Congo Crisis erupted in the summer of 1960 when a mutiny began in the army and Lumumba found himself dismissed as prime minister. He was now faced by his most effective opponent, Colonel Joseph-Desire Mobutu, who clearly had the backing of the USA.

Lumumba's position was increasingly perilous, and when letters and documents – some genuine, others forged – fell into Mobutu's hands the end was in sight. Lumumba might have denied it, but the documents clearly linked his party to communist USSR and China.

Lumumba was intercepted by state officials as he attempted to flee the country and join up with anti- Mobutu forces – the Free Republic of the Congo, as they called themselves – at Stanleyville. Beaten, kept on an almost non-existent diet, Lumumbu and two colleagues were held in captivity while a decision was reached regarding their fate. They were finally taken from the Congo, now called Zaire, to the breakaway state of Katanga.

Mobutu proclaimed that he had achieved 'a peaceful revolution', but it was clear that Lumumba would continue to be a thorn in his side. With American, British and Belgian approval, it was time for the final act. Lumumba and his two colleagues were taken to a remote part of the country, bound to trees and assassinated on 17 January 1961 by three separate firing squads, one after the other.

Patrice Lumumba was immediately made into a martyr for Pan-African movements across the continent. His death removed a problem for the CIA, MI6 and Belgium, who all had assassination plans in place. It did not, however, absolve them from guilt.

Ngo Diah Diem, South Vietnam (assassinated 2 November 1963)

Once the French pulled out of their colonial possession of Vietnam, the country became the location of the most significant conflict of the twentieth century between Western powers and communism. Central to the early part of the conflict was the South Vietnamese politician, Ngo Diah Diem.

Diem came from a Catholic family and for a while considered going into the Church as a career. He eventually became a civil servant and rose to the position of prime minister (1954–1955), and then, between 1955 and 1963, occupied the role of first President of the Republic of Vietnam. His promotions probably owed as much to a lack of effective opposition than it did to any specific skills Diem might have possessed.

A great believer in Vietnamese nationalism, Diem was supported by the USA and other anti-communist states. From the start, he needed that assistance as his regime found itself under intense pressure from communist insurgents led by Ho Chi Minh. A guerrilla-style campaign by the communists from the northern part of the country, a group later banded together as the Viet Cong, exposed many of the inadequacies of Diem's regime:

'With its unstable and incompetent government, South Vietnam would have been overrun, but as this was the major conflict in the Cold War with Russia, America could not simply abandon it to its fate.'[1]

By 1 November 1963, Diem was in desperate straits, facing attacks from the Viet Cong and insurgents or rebels from within his own territories. He was forced to turn once more to the Americans; he had nowhere else to go

Diem began pleading once more with Henry Cabot Lodge Jnr, the American Ambassador in Vietnam, for further support. This was refused, and an attack by rebellious generals on the Presidential Palace led only to a US offer of safe conduct out of South Vietnam. New US President John F. Kennedy was aware of the situation, but all the advice he was given was simply to leave well alone. Diem was not worth breaking sweat over.

The attack on the palace, supported by the CIA – whose officers had finally recognized the incompetence of the government – was successful. However, Diem and his brother, Nhu, managed to escape. The Americans would have undoubtedly preferred to see them captured or killed.

The two brothers took refuge in a Catholic church, but two days later realized the game was up. Diem told Ho Chi Minh that he would surrender, and an armoured car was sent to the church to pick up the South Vietnam leaders. At a railway crossing, the armoured car stopped and both Diem and Nhu were shot dead.

American officials rejoiced – surreptitiously. The assassination of Ngo Dinh Diem would, they believed, shorten American involvement in the war. That was their first reaction. However, opinions changed. Whether or not the CIA was behind the assassination has never been made clear, but it did mean that the American need to enforce a bulwark against communism ensured the continuation of the Vietnam War for some years to come, with the loss of tens of thousands of American lives once they became more involved in the conflict.

President John Fitzgerald Kennedy, Dallas, Texas (assassinated 22 November 1963)

The one assassination that almost everyone has heard about is that of American President John Fitzgerald Kennedy. JFK, as he was always known, was fatally struck by two bullets fired by an assassin – or assassins, depending on your viewpoint – on 22 November 1963.

The assassination, which occurred at 12.30 pm, shocked the entire world. It took place on Dealey Plaza in the Texas city of Dallas as Kennedy, seated alongside his wife, Jackie, and behind Texas Governor John B. Connolly, was being driven through the crowded streets in an open-topped car. It was, incidentally, the last time a US president travelled in an open-topped car.

Many people, in America and beyond, can still remember exactly where they were and what they were doing when they heard the news about Kennedy's assassination. Controversy about the shooting has raged ever since.

The youngest ever US president, just 46 when he died, Kennedy was a charismatic character. Almost by universal acclaim, he and his wife stood at the head of what was predicted to be a new age, a new era for America. His brief presidency has been called 'The New Camelot'. Assassination was the last thing on anyone's mind when the pair flew into Dallas that morning.

The alleged assassin was a man by the name of Lee Harvey Oswald, firing a cheap, bolt action carbine from a window on the sixth floor of the Texas School Book Depository where he worked. On investigation, it was stated that Oswald had fired three shots, two hitting JFK, a third missing altogether.

Despite considerable anti-Kennedy feeling in the city and specific advice from the Democratic Party HQ to cancel the visit, Kennedy had insisted the trip should go ahead. The American Nazi Party and the American Fact Finding Committee were both highly critical of JFK's determination to push through civil rights legislation which was designed to end racial segregation. There had been nearly 100 murders in the city that year, causing Kennedy to grin and announce to his wife: 'We're heading into nut country.'[2]

After the shooting, Oswald fled from the School Book Depository, leaving behind his rifle, presumably because it was unwieldy and likely to be noticed by the public. A palm print on the discarded rifle showed that it had been held and fired by Lee Harvey Oswald.

If we are to believe the Warren Commission investigation into the shooting, the first shot from Oswald's rifle had missed its mark, hitting a concrete pavement leading to a nearby underpass and chipping off a piece of concrete that cut into the cheek of a witness. President Kennedy was hit in the back of his neck by the second shot, the bullet coming out through his throat and going on to wound Governor Connally. The third shot was the most damaging and devastating, striking Kennedy in the back of the head and taking off most of his skull and the front part of the brain. Miraculously, Jackie Kennedy escaped any physical injury.[3]

JFK was rushed to hospital, but despite an emergency tracheotomy, within thirty minutes of his arrival he was pronounced dead. There was no thorough or intense autopsy, something that might have been expected in the case of an assassinated president and which might have given detailed evidence. There was only this very brief post-mortem. And then, at the request of Jackie Kennedy and JFK's brother, Bobby, the body was immediately flown to Washington on the presidential aircraft.

Lee Harvey Oswald was caught and arrested several hours later. In the interim period, he had taken a bus to the rooming house where he was living, picked up a revolver and then went out once more. Stopped by Dallas police patrol officer John Tippit, and in front of several witnesses, Oswald drew the loaded pistol and shot Tippit four times, killing him almost instantly.

Fleeing for a second crime, Oswald took refuge in a movie theatre. He had been seen entering the cinema and was soon approached by lawmen. Oswald tried to fire the revolver once again, but this time the gun misfired and he was taken into custody.

Police were never able to discover Oswald's motives, as he constantly proclaimed his innocence and insisted that he was a 'patsy' (i.e., a scapegoat). He was himself assassinated two days after Kennedy's death, gunned down live on TV by Jack Ruby in the basement of the Dallas Police headquarters. With his killing, the rumours and the deliberations of the conspiracy theorists really began.

Although the Warren Commission, called just a week after the fatal shooting of JFK to supposedly discover the facts of the assassination, concluded that Oswald was the assassin, it actually provided more questions than answers.

Those questions, left hanging over the affair, are still hovering and perplexing historians sixty years after Kennedy's death. Did Oswald really shoot Kennedy, and if so, was he acting alone? Was the CIA, KGB or Mafia involved? Was there an extra shooter lurking on the grassy knoll to the side of the president's motorcade? Three bullet casings were found in the Book Depository, so why did so many spectators claim they heard a fourth shot? The only useful film footage of the Kennedy assassination, taken by amateur photographer Abraham Zapruder, could be interpreted as proof of a second gunman. And so the questions go on.

In itself, Kennedy's death threw up many questions. Had he lived, would he have pulled American forces out of South Vietnam sooner rather than later? Lyndon Johnson, who succeeded Kennedy, went the other way, intensifying American involvement and spending millions of dollars – not to mention initiating a gross loss of life – in the process. It remains an imponderable.

One thing the assassination did achieve was to hurry civil rights legislation through the US legal system. This had already been wilfully obstructed in Congress, but the life of John F. Kennedy, it was argued, could be best honoured by pushing through that same legislation and making it law, resulting in the Civil Rights Act in the year after JFK's death.

Lee Harvey Oswald, Dallas, Texas (assassinated 24 November 1963)

Following his arrest on 22 November 1963, Lee Harvey Oswald was at first held in the Dallas City Jail. Two days later, as he was being moved to the County Jail, he was shot and killed by nightclub owner Jack Ruby.

To some extent, the killing of Oswald muddied the waters around President Kennedy's assassination. It took out the only person who had any real knowledge of what had gone on, leaving behind speculation and mystery. It remains, however, an important part of the whole affair.

Lee Harvey Oswald was just 24 years old when he was killed. He had led an unhappy childhood, his mother moving from one unfortunate relationship to another. A loner with no friends, he began committing minor criminal offences, which caused him to be sent to a US Correctional Facility for a brief period.

After dropping out of school, he joined the US Marines, achieving top marks in shooting and learning to speak Russian. Much to the chagrin of the Marine Corps, he made several public statements that he supported and firmly believed in the concept of communism.

Twice court martialled, Oswald was dishonourably dismissed from the Marines after turning up at the American Embassy in Moscow, where he swore his allegiance not to the United States of America but to the Soviet Union.

He defected to the USSR in 1959, marrying a Russian woman but being refused Russian citizenship. He was allowed to remain in the Soviet Union only as a resident alien. Surprisingly, in 1962, he, his wife and child were given permission to return to the USA.

He was angry about the dishonourable discharge, even writing to Governor Connally, giving rise to the conspiracy view that Connally was his real target, not JFK. Oswald flitted from one nondescript job to another, seeming to have no ambition or purpose in life – apart, his wife later said, from harbouring a desire to be famous. Good or bad, he didn't care which; he just wanted to be remembered.

On the morning of 24 November 1963, nightclub owner Jack Ruby made his way to the City Jail. His intention was to kill Oswald. The garage ramp along which Oswald was to come was crowded with dozens of spectators and pressmen. That in itself was a major safety hazard:

> 'I left Western Union and walked up Main Street toward the City Hall, not knowing the time they were about to transfer the man. I walked past them [guards and reporters] and I guess they didn't notice me. They were talking. I walked on down into the area where Oswald was being led out … I saw Oswald. I remember lunging at him. He was smirking and so cocky and acted so proud of what he had done.'[4]

Ruby's assassination of Oswald was caught by TV cameras. With his .38 calibre Colt pressed up against Oswald's stomach, there could be no doubt that Ruby had taken the law into his own hands.

Ruby's motives, as expressed by the man himself, seem to have changed several times, depending on his mood, the situation and the effect he wanted to achieve.

Firstly, he claimed to have done it so that Jackie Kennedy would not have to suffer the pressures of appearing in court. Then he said he did it as a simple act of revenge for Kennedy's assassination, because Oswald had 'killed his President' and needed to face the consequences of his action. He also said he did it because he did not believe that proper justice would be meted out by the US legal system.

Members of the press came up with their own rationale. It was said that Ruby had contacts with the mob and was the man charged with killing Oswald before he spilled out the truth. That truth, said the press, was that the assassination was organized and carried out by the US underworld.

Whatever the reason – and it was probably an amalgam of the above examples and more – when he faced trial, Ruby was found guilty and sentenced to death. This was later commuted to life imprisonment, and he died of lung cancer three years later in 1967.

Jack Ruby was mentally unbalanced, an unlikely mob hitman, but that did not prevent the world's press and the conspiracy theorists from coming up with a range of alternative motives, from KGB involvement to a plot by Vice-President Lyndon B. Johnson.

Malcolm X, Harlem, USA (assassinated 21 February 1965)

Malcolm X, whose birth name was Malcolm Little, also adopted for himself the name El Hajj Malik El-Shabazz (meaning, roughly, The Pilgrim Malcolm the Patriarch) after a pilgrimage to Mecca in 1964. To the world, however, he was known simply as Malcolm X, a title he had taken after casting off what he called the 'white slave master name' of Little.

He was a human rights activist and black nationalist, a self-educated former drug dealer and founder of the Organization of Afro-American Unity. In particular, Malcolm X was a major advocate of black empowerment and of the promotion of Islam within the black community. The separation of white and black Americans was an important issue for him.

Highly critical of civil rights proponents like Martin Luther King because of their opposition to the use of violence, Malcolm X was assassinated while giving a speech in the Audubon Ballroom in Harlem,

New York, on 19 May 1965. He died proclaiming to the last that he was not an American but a victim of the American system.

Born in Nebraska, Malcolm's father was a renowned evangelist and supporter of black human rights. The family received regular threats from organizations like the Ku Klux Klan and lived a nomadic sort of life. After the death of his father and hospitalization of his mother, Malcolm X spent most of his adolescence in foster homes. He gravitated to crime, eventually gaining himself an eight-year sentence for burglary, which was later extended to ten years for larceny.

While in prison, he joined the Nation of Islam. After his release, he became the public face of the organization for twelve years, reviled by white racists and moderate black activists because of his radical stance and support for violent responses to many of the country's problems. He was nothing if not outspoken, famously sounding off about the death of John F. Kennedy in *The New York Times* in December 1963:

> 'In further criticism of Mr Kennedy, the Muslim leader cited the murders of Patrice Lumumba, Congo leader, of Medgar Evers, civil rights leader, and of the negro girls bombed earlier in the year in a Birmingham church. These, he said, were instances of "chickens coming home to roost".'[5]

By the mid-1960s, however, Malcolm X had become disillusioned with the Nation of Islam, in particular with Elijah Muhammad, its leader. Over the next ten years or so, the relationship worsened, Malcolm X regularly receiving death threats from members of his old fraternity.

When looked at objectively, the life of Malcolm X seemed destined to end in tragedy. And that was exactly what happened on the afternoon of 21 February 1965. Speaking to an audience of 400, Malcom X was disturbed by shouts from the crowd. Verbal and racial abuse was followed by the scream 'Get your hand out of my pocket' from a man in the second row. A scuffle immediately broke out, Malcolm X calling out: 'Brothers, be cool.'

As his bodyguards tried to suppress the outburst, a smoke bomb went off at the back of the hall. At that moment, a man rushed forward, carrying a sawn-off shotgun which he fired into the chest of Malcolm X. The first attacker was quickly followed by two other assassins, who fired their automatic pistols into the slumped body of Malcolm X. When examined later in hospital, there were apparently 21 gunshot wounds along with countless shotgun pellets in his body.

The assassins attempted to flee the ballroom, but the crowd intervened. One of them, the shotgun wielder, was beaten half to death, his ankle broken and crippled with a gunshot wound in the thigh. The other two assassins suffered similar beatings.

The assassins were Thomas Hagan, Norman Butler and Thomas Johnson. All of them were members of the Nation of Islam and later changed their names, respectively, to Mujahid Abdul Halim, Muhammad Abdul Aziz and Khalil Islam. All three were sentenced to life imprisonment. The Nation of Islam denied any official involvement in the assassination, but three days after the killing, one of their mosques was burned to the ground.

Malcolm X was a controversial figure, accused of preaching his own brand of racism and violence. Now he is remembered and regarded as an icon, with streets named after him and Malcolm X Day celebrated in schools across the USA.

Henrik Verwoerd, Prime Minister of South Africa (assassinated 6 September 1966)

In the early afternoon of 6 September 1966, Henrik Verwoerd was stabbed to death by Dimitri Tsafendas while sitting in his seat in the South African Parliament House.

Regarded now as one of the architects of apartheid, Verwoerd was a bitter man with clear opinions and beliefs about the status of the white and black citizens of his country. His death shocked 'white South

Africa' but did nothing to halt or change the course of apartheid. If anything, it made the situation worse.

Verwoerd's policies, even after his death, ensured white and Afrikaner dominance in South Africa. It excluded the non-white majority of the populace from any type of involvement in or contribution to South African government or social life.

Under the government of Henrik Verwoerd, thousands of black South Africans were imprisoned – Nelson Mandela amongst them – and the country held the record for the largest number of executions, exiles and beatings in the Western world.

Verwoerd gave immense power to the police, granting them the right to stop, arrest and beat at will. Such power and control was used extensively and almost solely against the black members of South African society.

Verwoerd was in the process of turning South Africa into a republic when he was killed. The opposition of Britain, in particular, was anathema to Verwoerd. He was clear that total white supremacy was his goal and that Queen Elizabeth II had no influence in his country – she was simply the ruler of a hostile power.

Dimitri Tsafendas, his assassin, was an emotionally disturbed young man of Greek origin who was born in Mozambique in 1918. His father was a self-professed anarchist, and Tsafendas himself embraced communism. He had wanted to fight on the communist side during the Spanish Civil War, but never actually made it to Spain.

He spent the Second World War serving in the US Merchant Navy on convoys across the Atlantic. In 1947, he enrolled alongside the communist forces to fight in the Greek Civil War and then went to Rhodesia. He was deported from the latter country and, after a period wandering around Europe, wound up in South Africa in March 1965.

He had previously been denied entry to the country, but his family bribed customs officials in Mozambique, then a Portuguese colony, to grant him a visa. It would, the family thought, help him to settle down.

Despite considering and labelling Henrik Verwoerd as 'Hitler's best student', Tsafendas assured his family that he would behave himself in South Africa. He did not keep his promise for long.

When he began a temporary job as a parliamentary messenger, the proximity of Prime Minister Verwoerd was too great an opportunity to ignore. On 6 September 1966, he stabbed Verwoerd four times in the neck and chest before being wrestled to the floor by other members of parliament.

Tsafendas openly admitted that he had killed Verwoerd in an effort to destroy institutional racism in South Africa. In a statement made to the police but never used in court, Tsafendas was clear that the assassination of Verwoerd was an act of self-sacrifice on his part:

'I did believe that with the disappearance of the South African Prime Minister a change of policy would take place … It was my own idea to kill him. I did not care about the consequences.'[6]

Immediately arrested, Tsafendas was held in custody and tormented by the authorities by being kept on Death Row and repeatedly told that he would be executed unless he was declared insane. A mentally unbalanced assassin would be easier to explain away than any attempt to defend the defective protection system of apartheid. Tsafendas had already used the insanity plea to keep himself out of jail in Canada and the USA, and knew the effectiveness of such a claim.

He was soon declaring that he had a giant tapeworm in his stomach, compelling him to carry out the assassination. He was found not guilty on account of his madness or insanity, but was detained at the pleasure of the South African President. He survived for another thirty-three years, South Africa's longest-serving prisoner. He died in 1999, some years after the end of the apartheid system.

Martin Luther King, Civil Rights Campaigner, Memphis (assassinated 4 April 1968)

If anyone symbolized the 1960s and all it stood for, all that it promised and ultimately all that it failed to produce, it has to be civil rights activist Dr Martin Luther King. His assassination in 1968 was, in its own way, as memorable as that of John F. Kennedy. It was the death of a dream; not just Dr King's dream, but the hopes and desires of a whole nation.

It was perhaps inevitable that Martin Luther King would, sooner or later, fall victim to the violence and brutality he so deplored. The world knew it, and he knew it too.

When he spoke to a vast audience in Memphis on the night before his death, he was clear that he wanted a long life but was fearful that it would not happen. He had, he declared, seen the Promised Land, but 'I may not get there with you'. Prophetic, heart-rending, the phrase sums up King's life and work.

Trained and ordained as a pastor, Martin Luther King lived a life of protest and combat against racism. He began his career of protest by supporting the boycott of buses over segregation in Alabama, then moved on to opposing the Vietnam War. Equal wages for black people and a full-on anti-racist stance were the subjects of his many speeches.

He was constantly a target, soon the principal target, for various racist groups. The Ku Klux Klan bombed his house, while another property he had rented was riddled with bullets by an unknown gunman. His brother's house was bombed and King himself was stabbed in the chest by a mentally unbalanced woman, the blade just missing his heart. Death threats aimed at him and his family were common. Yet although death and destruction were constantly hovering, it did not stop Martin Luther King's avowed mission in life.

When, in April 1968, more than a thousand black refuse collectors and workers in Memphis went on strike for equal wages and recognition of their dangerous working conditions, King travelled to the city to support them in their fight. He spoke, as passionately as ever, to a huge audience, declaring that he had seen 'the glory of the coming of the Lord'.

The following evening, 4 April, Martin Luther King was shot as he stood on the balcony of the Lorraine Motel, one of the few hotels in Memphis that would take black people. The single bullet severed Dr King's jugular vein, shattered his cervical spine and caused other fatal injuries. The force of the shot threw him back against the wall and ripped off his collar and tie. He died in hospital an hour after the bullet struck him.

Quickly identifying the location from which the shot had come as a boarding house almost within spitting distance of King's motel, police found a Remington pump-action rifle, complete with telescopic sights. Fingerprints on the weapon and on other items identified the owner as James Earl Ray, a convicted criminal who had recently escaped from prison. Several fellow prisoners later alleged that whenever Ray saw Dr King on television, he would vow that, sooner or later, he was going to shoot the man.

There was no sign of Ray in the boarding house, but several witnesses claimed they had seen him run from the place and then drive furiously out of town. He was on the run for nearly a year before being apprehended at Heathrow Airport in London, preparing to board a plane to Brussels.

Since fleeing Memphis, Ray had been in Portugal and Canada, despite having no money or means of getting any. It was estimated that he would have needed nearly $10,000 to pay for his various trips and lifestyle.

The question that has never been answered is where all of that money came from. Ray claimed he had been given it by a blond-haired Cuban called Raoul who told him to buy the rifle and register as a guest in the boarding house.

The fatal shot was fired, Ray claimed, not by him but by Raoul, who dumped the rifle in the bathroom of the boarding house, where it was sure to be found by the Memphis police. Raoul was never identified or found.

The conspiracy theories were never as strong or as insistent as those surrounding the assassination of JFK, but they were still wide-ranging and wild. It was alleged that the Ku Klux Klan did it; that the Mafia, with interests in the waste disposal business, did it; that the Memphis police did it; even that J. Edgar Hoover hated King and ordered the FBI to eliminate him.

Various men were named as being involved in the assassination, but nothing was ever proved against them. Told he would face the death penalty if he pleaded not guilty and the judgement went against him, James Earl Ray admitted his guilt.

Sentenced to ninety-nine years in prison, he immediately recanted and proclaimed his innocence. He died, still in prison, in 1998. If anyone else was involved in the assassination of Dr King, then Ray took the secret with him to the grave.

Robert Francis Kennedy, former US Attorney General, Los Angeles (assassinated 6 June 1968)

Quite possibly the next US President, Robert Francis Kennedy, brother of JFK, was deprived of the opportunity when he was assassinated in the kitchen of the Ambassador Hotel, Los Angeles, on 6 June 1968.

Known almost universally as Bobby, Kennedy had served as attorney general for his brother but resigned when Lyndon Johnson chose Hubert Humphreys as his running mate in the forthcoming presidential elections. He was then elected as a senator in New York.

The new elections, set for November 1968, promised to be the hugely popular Bobby Kennedy's opportunity to follow in his brother's footsteps. But neither he nor anyone else realized that tragically, he would do exactly that.

Bobby Kennedy was the Democratic favourite to fight the forthcoming presidential election, but after his death things changed and Richard Nixon scored a narrow win for the Republicans.

Bobby's death came at a time when the USA was still reeling over the assassination of Martin Luther King, causing a wave of sorrow and discomfiture over the killing of the two Kennedy brothers.

Having delivered a speech to an ecstatic crowd of supporters, Kennedy's staff decided he would take a shortcut out of the Ambassador Hotel. He had just won the Californian Democratic Primary and his staff knew they had to get him away, as quickly as possible, from the adulation of the crowd.

The shortcut route took Bobby through the kitchens, where he came face to face with his killer, Sirhan Bishara Sirhan, a mentally deranged Palestinian who believed Kennedy's 'soft' approach towards Israel and the Jews would end in disaster. He had come to America with his parents in the 1950s while still a teenager, but never abandoned an interest in his Palestinian homeland.

The kitchen area was crowded with reporters, waiters and supporters. Bobby Kennedy, with his usual good humour, stopped to shake hands with almost everyone who offered their palms.

Sirhan suddenly appeared in front of him, brandishing a revolver. He fired eight times, only three of the bullets hitting Kennedy, one passing through his jacket, the others being wildly off target. Several people in the crowd were hurt by the wayward bullets, but all survived the shooting.

The bullet that hit Bobby Kennedy in the head caused serious and, as it turned out, fatal damage, severing the cerebral artery. Despite this, he was able to ask if everyone was all right before passing out.

Realizing the seriousness of the situation, a Catholic in the crowd administered the last rights and Bobby was whisked away to hospital. Treatment was swift but ineffective, and he died without regaining consciousness.

Sirhan was badly beaten by the crowd before being arrested. At his trial, he was found guilty of murder and sentenced to death. However, before the execution could be carried out the state of California abolished the death penalty and his sentence was commuted to life in prison. Allowed the right to appeal for parole, so far Sirhan has not been granted his freedom under this privilege.

As might be expected, questions still remain about the killing of Bobby Kennedy. Witnesses were sure that Sirhan fired at Kennedy from the front, yet an entrance wound was found on the back of the victim's neck, suggesting the possibility that there may have been a second assassin.

All eight bullets from Sirhan's gun were accounted for, but two additional holes, which might have been bullet holes, were later discovered in a wooden panel in the kitchen. Was that wrongly identified damage? Possibly.

Looking at the evidence, one is simply left with the notion that it would not have been an American assassination without some degree of confusion and doubt being left behind.

*   *   *

The assassination of Bobby Kennedy was the last really significant political killing of the 1960s. Individual killings like the 1969 murder of actress Sharon Tate and her friends caused huge press and public interest, but were not assassinations in the true sense of the word. Tate's murder was simply the fulfilling of a desire by Charles Manson's bizarre semi-religious cult. Nobody set out to kill Sharon Tate; she was simply in the wrong place at the wrong time.

Assassinations did not cease, however, and in the ten troubled years that followed on from the Sixties there were many other high-profile killings, notably in newly developed countries within Africa and in the troubled area of Latin or Central America.

Chapter Eight

On into the 1970s

After the wild excesses of the 1960s, the next decade was one of complete contrast. It was a period of economic and political diversity, an era that saw the Watergate Scandal, energy shortages, power cuts and the worldwide effects of decolonization. The Vietnam War might have ended, but other conflicts soon arose in the Middle East, Africa and Latin America to replace it.

The 1970s was an age of significant change. Women's rights became a long-overdue issue, as did debate and new laws centred around the gay community and the legalizing of homosexuality. Cultural diversity rose, amidst the boundaries of violence and ignorance, to be a central theme for many people.

The 1970s was an age of political coups, a dozen major upheavals at the point of a gun cementing the rise of Islam in countries such as Iran. Over ten years, the world's population increased dramatically and the digital age began. In Britain, the election of Margaret Thatcher saw the UK's first female prime minister, whose message was simple – you can have what you want when you want it; worry about paying for it later.

Assassination continued to be employed by political groups, many of them holding minority positions and opinions. In many respects, this was the era when terrorism really began to rear its ugly head. Fanatical belief eagerly seized on assassination as a cheap but effective way of making a point. The only real cost lay in the loss of life.

The Munich Massacre – Israeli Athletes at the Olympic Games, Munich (multiple assassinations, 5 and 6 September 1972)

The world was shocked when, on the night of 5 September 1972, a terrorist attack was launched on Israeli competitors at the Munich Olympic Games. The Israeli targets of the attack, along with the West German police, were unsuspecting and unprepared. The perpetrators of what became known as the Munich Massacre were members of the Palestinian Black September Movement.

Eight terrorists infiltrated the Olympic Village, killing two members of the Israeli athletics team in the process. They moved on to take a further nine athletes and coaches as prisoners or hostages. They then demanded the release of over 200 prisoners, mostly members of the Baader Meinhof Gang, who were currently being held in Israeli and West German prisons.

The real purpose behind the attack was not to force the release of prisoners but to draw attention to the Palestinian situation in the Holy Land. Luttif Afif, commander of the eight-man terrorist squad, was clear that he and his comrades might die in the attack, but so too would the Israeli competitors.

A total lack of awareness on behalf of the West Germans saw a rescue attempt fail. Holed up in the athletes' quarters, the Black September terrorists were able to track the rescue attempt by watching German news programmes on television. Nobody thought of closing down the service.

Although five of the terrorists were eventually killed, all of the hostages suffered the same fate. Two helicopters sent in to airlift the terrorists and hostages to Furstenfeld airfield proved to be death traps once the members of Black September realized that the Lufthansa aircraft they had demanded had no fuel and no crew. It was no more than a decoy.

Hand grenades and machine-gun fire from the terrorists brought sniper fire from the police. In the end, casualty figures were high.

Along with the two original fatalities when the Black September killers forced their way into the Olympic Village, five Israeli athletes, six of their coaches and one West German policeman were killed. Five of the terrorists, including Luttif Afif, were shot dead and three others arrested. They were released within a month as part of a prisoner exchange following the highjacking of Lufthansa Flight 615.

The terrorist attack on what was supposedly a peaceful gathering of athletes and fans shocked everyone. It was the start of a prolonged and vicious series of assassinations as minority groups tried to influence stronger and more powerful opponents.

Victor Jara, singer/songwriter, Chile (assassinated 16 September 1973)

Victor Lidio Jara Martinez was born in the rural wilds of Chile in 1932. His father was an illiterate tenant farmer who saw no purpose behind education, expecting his six sons to help him farm the land. His wife could read and write; that was more than enough to get by. She also played guitar and piano, skills which she happily passed on to young Victor.

When Jara's father turned to drink, he would often spend weeks away from the family, a situation that pleased everyone. Jara's mother moved to Santiago, where she worked as a cook in a successful restaurant. She died when Victor was just 15, leaving him virtually alone in the world.

Luckily for him, Jara's mother had given him the basics of education – along with skills in music and singing – and he began to study, firstly as an accountant and then for the priesthood. His real love, however, was for poetry and song, and he did not finish his course.

After some time in the Chilean Army, he enrolled at university, where he began to really develop his musical talents. He sang in the choir and immersed himself in Chilean musical traditions. His first album, heavily laden with Chilean influences, came out in 1966 to a rapturous reception.

Heavily influenced by the poet Pablo Neruda, Jara was soon making a name for himself as a proponent of the new Chilean Song Movement. Always interested in politics and social justice, Jara was a firm supporter of President Salvador Allende, something he was happy to announce to the world. Before long, he became a cultural ambassador for Allende and his left-wing regime.

In an era of revolt and rebellion, his support for people such as Che Guevara, hero of the Cuban revolution, combined with his writing and music, brought Jara increasing international recognition.

As a confirmed communist, Jara seemed to have a knack for annoying and offending conservative elements in the higher echelons of Chilean government. In the dark and dangerous world of Chilean society, he was a target for assassins from the mid-1960s until his death in 1973. It was something that Jara accepted as a fact of life. More than once, he was beaten up by right-wing thugs, but his belief in social and political reform kept him going.

Jara's life as a singer/songwriter, poet, theatre director and, increasingly, as a political activist soon made him into a cult figure – and not just in Chile.

A song he wrote concerning a deeply religious woman who fell in love with the local priest was banned and removed from circulation in Chile. Jara did not mind; he was making his talents known and respected in an increasingly wide circle, particularly the USA, where singers and writers like Bob Dylan and Joan Baez had become admirers.

On 11 September 1973, a coup led by Augusto Pinochet, supported by an increasingly paranoid US government, overthrew President Allende. That same evening, Jara was arrested. He was tortured during his later interrogation, one story telling of an army officer who threw down a cigarette end and forced Jara to pick it up. He then stamped on Jara's hands, ruining forever his ability as a guitarist. It hardly mattered as Jara did not survive the night.

He was shot in the back of his head and then forty machine-gun bullets were pumped into his body. His corpse was strung up as an example to others, then torn down and flung out into the streets of a shanty town suburb of Santiago. His songs, focussing as they did on peace and social justice, ensured that his name and reputation would survive such indignities:

> '[He was] a potent symbol of struggle for human rights and justice for those killed during the Pinochet regime.'[1]

Victor Jara was typical of the politically minded folk singers who came to prominence during the Sixties and Seventies. As a social and political activist, as well as a songwriter of considerable skill, he remains right up there alongside the likes of Bob Dylan and Pete Seeger.

Sheikh Mujibur Rahman, President of Bangladesh (assassinated 15 August 1975)

The historic region of Bengal in north-eastern India became part of Pakistan when the sub-continent was partitioned in 1947. Separated from the rest of Pakistan by the rapidly drawn Radcliffe Line, as well as by culture, history and several thousand miles of Indian territory, the relationship between East Pakistan, as the region was now declared, and the rest of the new nation was never an easy partnership.

Failure by the Pakistani government to act quickly after a devastating cyclone in 1970 was a turning point for the people of East Pakistan, or Bangladesh as it is now known. The cyclone caused a tragedy, with half-a-million deaths and many more people displaced and made homeless. It was an event that caused unprecedented anger in East Pakistan.

The cyclone preceded the 1971 elections, where the people showed their displeasure by returning nearly 100 per cent of the radical, independence-minded Awami League members. Mass civil demonstrations evolved into war and East Pakistan, along with its newly discovered Indian allies, fought for and gained independence.

Sheikh Mujibur Rahman, leader of the Awami League, was installed as prime minister in 1972. Politically active since the creation of Pakistan, Mujibur had led many protests against the original Pakistani regime, and had consequently spent several periods in jail. He was accused at various times of being an agent for India or a secessionist. As Prime Minister of Bangladesh, he became renowned as the Father of the Nation, having led the region of Bengal to independence for the first time since Robert Clive's victory for Britain and the East India Company at the Battle of Plassey in 1757.

His job was far from easy. For the next few years, the People's Republic of Bangladesh suffered from famine, poverty and the standard growing pains of almost all newly created nations.

Sheikh Mujibur was aware of a steadily increasing displeasure in the country. Partly as a result of this festering anger, Mujibur's political stance changed and hardened, and he gradually became more autocratic. Originally founded on the British concept of democratic government, Bangladesh had, by the summer of 1975, become a one-party socialist state, with Mujibur now installed as president.

On the evening of 15 August 1975, a coup by dozens of disgruntled army officers, ranging from colonels to the lowest subalterns, toppled Sheikh Mujibur's regime. They stormed into the president's private residence and shot not just Mujibur but his whole family and any staff or servants they could find in the building. Two of Mujibur's daughters were lucky to survive the coup, being away in Germany at the time.

Mujibur himself was discovered on the staircase of the house and mercilessly shot down. The presidency passed to a series of usurpers, Ziaur Rahman being the most notable.

Ziaur, like several before him, was assassinated before his term was up. In an increasingly violent and troubled nation, Sheikh Hasina, daughter of Mujibur, became president in 2009, managing to bring some sort of political stability to a troubled nation.

The assassination of Sheikh Mujibur Rahman did not achieve anything like the stability and security that the rebellious army officers had hoped to create. Instead, it led to increased violence and the genocide of many thousands.

Ross McWhirter, TV Personality, Enfield, London (assassinated 27 November 1975)

For most of the British public, the 1970s were dominated by what were known as the Troubles in Ireland. A rampant IRA, divided from 1969 into the Provisional and the Official Irish Republican Armies, took the fight for Irish independence out of the home country and began a series of offensives in mainland Britain.

In a fourteen-month terror campaign, thirty-five people in Britain were killed in bomb attacks, with many more injured. Assassinations, bombings and other, terrorist attacks dominated the headlines, none more so than the killing of TV personality and journalist Ross McWhirter on 27 November 1975.

Ross and his twin brother, Norris, were sports journalists who, in 1955, produced the first Guinness Book of Records. They became TV personalities thanks to their appearances on shows such as *Record Breakers*.

Ross McWhirter was a right-wing conservative who was outspoken about the Irish Troubles and the way they should be managed. He launched a 'Beat the Bombers' campaign, promising a substantial reward for the conviction of IRA bombers, and went on to suggest that all Southern Irish nationals living in Britain should have to register with the police.

Ross McWhirter knew that his stance was likely to provoke a response. He claimed that he was on the IRA death list, but continued to condemn the bombers for their campaign. Whether or not he was on a death list, he eventually met his end on 27 November 1975.

Harry Duggan and Hugh Docherty, two IRA gunmen, waited in the garden of McWhirter's house in Enfield, north London. When they knocked on the front door, Ross McWhirter answered and they shot him. The death of a 'celebrity' marked a new phase in the IRA campaign. It caused a brief and immediate outrage, doing little to help the IRA cause.

Duggan and Docherty were part of the IRA gang that had hurled a bomb through Scott's restaurant in Soho. The bombing harmed no-one and led to the eventual capture of the gang after what became known as the Balcombe Street Siege.

Steve Biko, Black Activist and Human Rights Worker, South Africa (assassinated 12 September 1977)

Although Steve Biko was only 30 when he died, he had established a reputation as a fierce fighter for human rights in a country where apartheid was law and to be born black was to be relegated to third- or fourth-class citizenship.

Expelled from his first high school because of his political activism, Biko enrolled at and later graduated from St Francis College, a boarding school in Natal. He then went to study at the University of Natal Medical School, where he became involved with the multiracial National Union of South African Students, a moderate organization with which he soon became disenchanted. The union, he said, needed to be remodelled around the culture of a black majority.

In 1968, Biko was a founder member of the all-black South African Students Organization, becoming its first president the following year. Central to his thinking was the concept of black consciousness, something that manifested itself in helping people recognize their self-worth and, in consequence, their dignity as human beings.

Steve Biko's writings and speeches were radical, regarded by many as racist and anti-white. It was, however, a stance that Biko and many other activists knew had to be made if the black people of South Africa were to be accepted as equal.

One of the founders of the Black People's Convention, Biko was active throughout the Seventies and jailed many times for his actions.

On at least four occasions he was held in custody for several months, without trial or charges being brought against him. He knew the difficult and dangerous course he was running, but as he stated, 'Black man, you are on your own.'

In 1973, he and the BPC organization were restricted in their movements and in expressing their political beliefs. Biko was confined to the King William Town district, forbidden to speak to more than one person at a time. The press were forbidden to quote him in any article or broadcast.

Steve Biko's house in Ginsberg was a regular target for racist attacks, gun shots often being aimed at the building from cars that sped past. A group of young supporters, calling themselves The Cubans, was formed to protect him, showing the support he had garnered from the black youth of the country. The South African government, firm in their belief in apartheid, had long considered him a nuisance. Now he was downright dangerous and a clear threat to the racist regime.

Despite all this, Biko continued to work. Amongst other activities, he covertly established the Zimele Trust Fund to help political prisoners and their families.

On 18 August 1977, he and several members of the Convention were stopped by security police at a roadblock. They were on their way back from a fruitless meeting in Cape Town with the leader of the Unity movement. Biko and his comrades having broken their restriction order, the police eagerly seized the offenders.

Biko was held in the Port Elizabeth police station before being moved to the government security headquarters, where he was repeatedly and ruthlessly beaten. His treatment and subsequent death – after many days of violence on the part of the authorities – were carefully thought out by South African police and security forces. It was assassination of a different sort, but however it is looked at it was certainly a political killing.

Held naked and shackled by his legs, at one stage he was forbidden to sit and was forced to remain standing erect in a tiny cell with his arm protruding from the window. Now desperately ill, he was bundled into the back of a police Landover and taken on an 800-mile trip to hospital in Pretoria, where doctors claimed they could see nothing wrong with him.

On 12 September 1977, Steve Biko died as a result of the severe beatings he had received. Blood cells had apparently entered his spinal fluid, but police and security services were cleared of any criminal behaviour. The news of his death was reported in succinct but unemotional articles in the world's press:

'Black activist Steve Biko dies in South African prison cell … The founder of the Black Consciousness Movement had been hailed as one of the country's most important politicians.'[2]

Somewhere in the region of 20,000 people attended Biko's funeral, many more being denied participation by the South African security services. It was a monumental moment in the history of South Africa, but it was still nearly twenty years before apartheid was abolished and Nelson Mandela, himself a long-term political prisoner, became the first black president of the country.

Now, 27 April – the date of the first totally free and equal elections with black and white citizens casting a vote – is recognized as Freedom Day in South Africa. The tragedy is that although Steve Biko's assassination contributed to the end of an evil system, he was not there to see it.

Georgi Markov, Bulgarian Writer, Playwright and Dissident, London (assassinated 11 September 1978)

It is difficult to categorize the death of Georgi Markov – political assassination, a revenge murder or perhaps a little bit of both? He died after being stabbed with a poisoned umbrella while waiting for a bus on Waterloo Bridge in London. It was 7 September 1978 and the killing was just like something out of a James Bond novel.

A hugely successful Bulgarian playwright, Markov defected to the West, seeking asylum in England, when his latest play was banned by the Bulgarian government. Bulgarian President Todor Zhivkov was little more than a Soviet puppet and Markov was not slow to criticize the man and his regime, both before and after his defection.

Settling in London, Markov broadcast regularly for the BBC's World Service and for Radio Free Europe. His broadcasts, vicious and totally unrestrained, were largely about Bulgaria and the apparatchiks who ran the country:

'His wife said that his comments on the communist elite in Bulgaria were "vitriolic" and with his comments on their sex lives he was smearing mud on the people in the inner circle.'[3]

President Zhivkov, in particular, came in for severe criticism from the exiled writer. Never one to cope with criticism at any level, Zhivkov asked for Russian help in dealing with Markov. Two KGB agents duly arrived in Bulgaria, carrying ricin poison which was held in a wax-coated pellet no bigger than a pin head and then lodged in an umbrella tip. The build-up to the assassination had begun.

On 7 September, while standing in a London bus queue, an unsuspecting Georgi Markov felt a sudden sharp pain, like a bee or wasp sting, in his thigh. Mumbling an apology, a passer-by with an umbrella strode away, then leapt into a taxi and disappeared.

Markov found only a tiny red scratch on his leg, but within hours he developed a fever. He died four days after being jabbed with the umbrella tip. A small pellet containing ricin was found in his body, but although the KGB later admitted their involvement, the assassin was never discovered.

Russian use of poison as an assassination tool did not begin or end with the death of Georgi Markov. In August 1978, another Bulgarian defector, Vladimir Kostov, survived a ricin attack, while in 2006, Alexander Litvinenko was killed by polonium poisoning. There have probably been many more such incidents.

Airey Neave, politician, London (assassinated 30 March 1979)

Airey Neave was a man of many parts. A soldier, an Intelligence Officer for the British Army, a barrister and a Member of Parliament, he was also a great supporter and friend of Margaret Thatcher. In March 1979, he became the first high-profile victim of the Irish bombing campaign since Ross McWhirter several years before.

He was assassinated by the Irish National Liberation Army on 30 March 1979 when they planted a bomb under his car. As he was driving out of the Palace of Westminster, the bomb exploded, blowing off Neave's legs and causing other severe injuries that led to his death half an hour after he was pulled from his shattered car.

A war hero of some note, Airey Neave was captured by the Germans during the British retreat to Dunkirk in 1940. After several escape attempts, he wound up at Colditz Castle, where 'troublesome' prisoners were housed. He escaped twice from Colditz, the second attempt leading him to Switzerland and freedom. He was the first British officer to achieve this feat during the war.

Returned to active duty, Neave became an Intelligence Officer for MI9 and, with the war over, served on the Military Tribunal at the Nuremberg Trials for war crimes.

Upon demobilization, he became a barrister but his heart and ambition lay in politics. A staunch conservative, after two failed attempts Neave finally became MP for Abingdon. However, he saw his prospects stall after a heart attack in 1959. Ted Heath told him that his career was over, but Neave was not a man to take notice of such advice. He continued as a Member of Parliament.

He was a staunch supporter of Margaret Thatcher and acted as her campaign manager when she fought and won the nomination for leader of the Conservative Party. Thatcher rewarded Neave by making him Secretary of State for Northern Ireland.

As Secretary of State, he was adamant that the government should abandon its policy of containment regarding terrorist groups in Ireland and switch to one that sought political and military defeat for groups such as the INLA and the IRA. His stance infuriated the INLA in particular, making him a marked man.

His assassination came just a few weeks before the 1979 General Election which saw the Conservative Party and Margaret Thatcher installed at Number Ten. There were more assassinations and more killings to come as part of the Irish Troubles.

Lord Mountbatten, Mullaghmore Harbour, Ireland (assassinated 27 August 1979)

Louis Mountbatten, Earl Mountbatten of Burma, is best remembered as the man who, as the last Viceroy of India, oversaw the end of the British Raj.

He had led an active and interesting war, commanding destroyers and, lastly, an aircraft carrier in the fight against Hitler's Germany. In the immediate post-war years, he went on to become Admiral of the Fleet.

A member of the Royal family, Mountbatten was godfather and mentor to Prince (now King) Charles. A great grandson of Queen Victoria, on 27 August 1979 he became the most renowned victim of the IRA bombing campaign.

He and his family took regular holidays at his house in Mullaghmore, County Sligo, just a few miles from the border with Northern Ireland. This was 'bandit country', and Mountbatten was putting himself at risk every time he went there. However, he ignored advice from the police and the military and continued to take regular breaks in his Irish house.

He was particularly fond of sailing, his fishing boat *Shadow V* being moored in Mullaghmore's harbour. There was no specific security around the boat, Mountbatten believing that his popularity with the locals would keep him safe. Tragically, he was wrong.

On the night of 26 August, a 50lb bomb, to be detonated by remote control, was planted on the *Shadow V.* An earlier attempt to shoot Mountbatten had been cancelled because of bad weather and choppy seas. The use of a bomb offered an altogether more likely chance of success.

The assassin was an IRA man by the name of Thomas McMahon. He had crept aboard the unguarded vessel under cover of darkness in order to plant and arm the bomb. The following day, as Mountbatten and his family set out from Mullaghmore harbour, the bomb was triggered by an accomplice of McMahon. It destroyed the boat, instantly killing Lord Mountbatten.

He was not the only victim. Mountbatten's grandson, Nicholas, aged just 15, also died on the boat, along with the young boat hand, Paul Maxwell. Mountbatten's daughter, the Dowager Lady Brabourne, died later from her injuries at Sligo General Hospital.

The IRA admitted responsibility for the deaths, claiming that the assassination of Lord Mountbatten and the others was simply to draw people's attention to what they called 'the occupation' of their country.

By pure chance, two hours before the detonation of the bomb, Thomas McMahon was arrested by police. The arrest had nothing to do with the coming assassination.

Police originally suspected McMahon of driving a stolen car, but soon, as forensic investigation began to pick up traces of nitro-glycerine and specks of paint from the *Shadow V* on his clothing, the more grievous charge of murder was brought against him. He was sentenced to life imprisonment, but was later released as part of the Good Friday Agreement.

The IRA tried to justify the assassination of Lord Mountbatten by claiming that they had done to him exactly what he had spent his life doing to others. It was a spurious argument, and the assassination caused shock throughout the world. Even Irish-Americans, previously unshakeable in their views and unstinting support of the Republican cause, were taken aback by the assassination.

On the same day as they assassinated Lord Mountbatten, IRA bombers and assassins murdered eighteen British soldiers. The attack, which became known as the Warrenpoint Ambush, was a brutal affair.

From the IRA point of view, the Warrenpoint Ambush was the most successful attack on British Army personnel since the Troubles began. The murder of Lord Mountbatten was equally as high profile, indeed the highest-profile action attempted so far.

For the British government, the two incidents were proof that the IRA was not just a bunch of amateur patriots. This was, effectively, war, and if it was a conflict that going to be won then a more professional approach was required. The war against the Irish terrorists consequently went up several notches.

Chapter Nine

Final Acts of Assassination in the Twentieth Century

The final two decades of the twentieth century saw no let-up in the number of assassinations that had bedevilled the modern world for the previous eighty years. Politicians continued to be a primary target, but they were not alone. The range of victims now broadened to take in people like actors, sportsmen and singers.

Musicians such as Victor Jara had been shot and killed in the previous decades, but such victims usually had some form of political connections or interest; if ever there was a case of the singer bowing to the strength of the song, that was surely it. Now, in the Eighties, singers and composers such as John Lennon, who had only fringe involvement with politics, or Marvin Gaye, who had almost none at all, became assassination targets for very little reason other than their wealth and fame.

People like the fashion designer Gianni Versace, actor Sal Mineo and even Pope John Paul II found themselves at risk as assassins – successfully or not – attempted to end their lives. It's hard to believe, but Joseph Stalin had once ordered the assassination of John Wayne and even sent two agents to the USA to carry out the attack. Needless to say, the attempted murder failed dismally.

American rap and hip-hop musicians – at least two dozen of them – were a prime target. Several of the assassinated artists had connections with the criminal underworld, some were involved in the drug scene, while others were killed simply because they had become rich and famous. Intolerance and jealousy were now major factors – 'they've got it, I want it', as someone once declared.

John Lennon, Singer/Songwriter, New York (assassinated 8 December 1980)

John Lennon, founder member of The Beatles, was perhaps the most influential singer and songwriter of the Sixties and Seventies. By 1980, he had moved on from the mop-top generation. He had left the Beatles, divorced his first wife, married the artist Yoko Ono and was living in the Dakota Building in New York City.

Lennon loved New York. He could walk the streets without being mobbed and lived a life of virtual anonymity amongst the hurrying crowds. He could happily write his songs, record his albums and return each night to the luxury of his apartment in the Dakota. Perhaps for the first time in his life, he was thoroughly, completely content.

Enter Mark David Chapman. A disgruntled, unfulfilled young man in his early 20s, Chapman was an acknowledged fan of The Beatles and of J.D. Salinger's novel *The Catcher in the Rye*. The hero of Salinger's book is Holden Caulfield, someone who despises hypocrisy and people whom he regards as 'phonies'. Chapman identified with Holden Caulfield and based his whole life around the fictional character's personality.

In his song *Imagine*, Lennon had asked his public to conjure for themselves a world of no religion and no wars. Much to Chapman's fury, he also asked his listeners, whoever they might be, to 'Imagine no possessions" And yet Lennon was living in luxury in the Dakota. To Chapman, that was the ultimate phoney stance. And wasn't it John Lennon who, in 1966, had proclaimed that The Beatles were more popular than Jesus? In Chapman's mind, it all mounted up – phoney, phoney, phoney.

The more he thought about it, the angrier and more jealous Chapman became. Lennon's success prodded constantly at his brain. 'I was so compelled to commit the murder,' Chapman later remarked.[1] Driven by a combination of betrayal and disgust, he took seven months to plan what he would do.

He bought a gun, a cheap five-shot .38 revolver, flew from Hawaii, where he was living, and on 8 December 1980 found himself clutching Lennon's *Double Fantasy* album and standing with other fans outside the Dakota. He spent most of the day there until, just after 5.00 pm, John Lennon, on his way to the recording studio, came out of the building. He signed the record sleeve, spoke to Chapman briefly and went off to complete his evening's work.

Mark Chapman was still there when Lennon returned at 11.15 pm. As the singer passed him, Chapman pulled out his revolver and fired five times at his target. Four of the bullets smashed into Lennon's shoulder and back. Chapman stood calmly by as Lennon was rushed to hospital in a police car. He began to turn the pages of his copy of *Catcher in the Rye*, studying each one until he was finally arrested. Meanwhile, Lennon was pronounced dead on arrival at the hospital.

Chapman's behaviour after the shooting highlighted his mental instability. At no stage did he attempt to flee the scene or deny assassinating John Lennon. He even admitted the crime when asked by the Dakota doorman if he knew what he had done. Throughout his murder trial and all his subsequent imprisonment, he took a contradictory, even puzzling, view of the man he had killed:

'He was very kind to me … he took his time with me and he got the pen going and signed my album. He asked me if I needed anything else. I said "No, no sir." And he walked away. A very cordial and decent man.'[2]

Nevertheless, this cordiality and decency did not stop John Lennon from becoming the victim of a highly disturbed and dangerous young man who had chosen to base his life on the main character from a work of fiction. Chapman had compiled a list of alternative or future targets, with David Bowie and Elizabeth Taylor featuring prominently. He later declared that the only rationale behind appearing on the list was their fame.

Debate and discussion about the state of Chapman's mental health eventually ended with the judgement that he was sane enough to stand trial. He was sentenced to between twenty years and life in prison. He has since made a dozen appeals against his conviction, but remains in custody. Thousands mourned John Lennon, and there were at least three suicides in the wake of his death – a tragic story all around.

Anwar Sadat, President of Egypt, Cairo (assassinated 6 October 1981)

Succeeding Colonel Gamal Abdel Nasser as President of Egypt in 1970, Anwar Sadat was a man with a clear vision of what was needed if his country was to survive and thrive in the turmoil of Middle East politics. His vision and viewpoint meant that he was also a political leader who presented the world with a wide-open target for assassination.

A soldier, politician and veteran of Egypt's fight for independence from Britain, Anwar Sadat led his country into the Yom Kippur War of 1973. The conflict saw Egypt, for the first time, retake recently conquered territory from Israel when Sadat's forces crossed the Suez Canal into the Sinai Peninsula to claim back land they had lost in the 1967 war.

Sadat was no warmonger, however, and from the end of the Yom Kippur War he worked hard to achieve a degree of reconciliation with his northern neighbours. In 1979, Egypt became the first Arab nation to sign a peace treaty with Israel, an act that saw Sadat, along with Israeli Prime Minister Menachem Begin, awarded the Nobel Peace Prize.

However, the peace was fragile and was not achieved without cost. Anti-Sadat groups voiced their disaffection with the way Egypt was 'giving in' to Israel, and that, combined with a downturn in the Egyptian economy, helped create a mood of bitter unhappiness in the country. Sadat was the target of much scorn and anger, not just within his own country but from most of the Arab world. Egypt was suspended from the Arab League and, as hostility increased, Sadat found himself forced to take an increasingly authoritarian stance. Parliament was suspended and strikes by labour groups were banned.

On 6 October 1981, Anwar Sadat attended a celebratory parade and display to mark the eighth anniversary of the Yom Kippur War and the reclaiming of the Sinai Peninsula. It was to be a display of strength by the Egyptian Army and Sadat felt he would be safe attending the celebration. He could not have been more mistaken.

As a flight of Mirage jets from the Egyptian Air Force swept overhead, everyone on the parade ground raised their eyes to follow their progress – including Sadat's bodyguards. A lorry full of supporters of the Muslim Brotherhood then came to a halt in front of the viewing platform where Sadat was standing. Four assassins, led by Lieutenant Khalid El-Islambouli, leapt out of the truck and raced towards the president.

Three hand grenades were thrown, but only one exploded. Then the assassins opened fire with machine guns and AK47 rifles. Before they knew what was happening, Sadat and others around him were raked by bullets.

Anwar Sadat, who went to his death believing that this was part of the parade, stood to attention and saluted his attackers. Then he was hit by four bullets and fell to the ground. Alert watchers tried to protect him by covering his body with chairs. It was to no avail; he died in hospital two hours later.

More soldiers leapt from the truck and added to the chaos. They continued to pour gunfire into the crowd until their ammunition was exhausted. Then they attempted to flee, but the Egyptian security forces were now alert. They killed two of the assassins and captured the others. Five of the assassins were later tried and executed. In an attack that lasted just two minutes, Sadat and two of his ministers were killed. The death toll eventually rose to eleven.

The assassination had been planned and carried out by the Muslim Brotherhood, a radical organization intending to establish a Fundamentalist Muslim government. They had to wait another twenty years for that. After the assassination, Sadat's deputy, Hosni Mubarak, took control, reinforcing and protecting the Egyptian government by military strength. Eventually, and after several attempts at assassination, Mubarak was overthrown by the Brotherhood.

Indira Gandhi, Indian Prime Minister, New Delhi (assassinated 31 October 1984)

Indira Gandhi, daughter of Jawaharlal Nehru, served two terms as Prime Minister of India. Her accession to leadership was an unusual event in a country that took for granted the stance of male dominance, with women working or using whatever powers they might possess behind the scenes rather than in the limelight.

Indira Gandhi might have been the first female leader of her country, but from the start she displayed a firmness that shocked many of her male counterparts. Her second period in office began in January 1980 and was cut short when she was assassinated on 31 October 1984.

Mrs Gandhi's two periods in power came at a difficult time for what was still the embryonic country of India. Independence from Britain had only come about in 1947 and the country was still bedevilled by the clashes between religious groupings that had marred the initial independence celebrations. External issues were just as significant and just as violent.

War with Pakistan, ongoing debates about Kashmir, border disputes with China and many other warlike incidents had haunted the country throughout the early years of its existence. They were just the tip of the iceberg. The various conflicts were conducted within the economic chaos caused by a devaluation of the rupee which ruined many Indian businesses and caused widespread poverty across the nation.

Far more troubling for Indira Gandhi, however, was a growing Sikh desire for autonomy and the creation of a Sikh state in the Punjab region of the country. Mrs Gandhi, a firm believer in the maintenance of a single united India, adopted a hard authoritarian line with all those who wanted to separate or split away from the main country. In hindsight, it was a dispute that was almost certain to end in conflict.

In 1982, 200 Sikhs took control of the Golden Temple at Amritsar in the Punjab. The Golden Temple was the most holy shrine of the Sikh religion, but the rebellious occupiers of the building began to adapt it so that it became, literally, a fortress. As debate and discussion between Indira Gandhi and the Sikh religious leaders went on, many more Sikhs swarmed into the Golden Temple to take up arms against the Indian government.

Finally, in 1984, Gandhi lost patience and ordered the Indian Army to storm the stockade. Despite the Army's use of tanks and artillery, the Sikhs fought back desperately and bravely, leading to seven days of brutal conflict.

Reports on casualty figures vary, some sources stating that around 5,000 Sikh militants were killed, others putting the figure at 20,000. Some reports say that Army casualties were as low as 100, others recording a death toll in the thousands. Regardless of how many died, the Golden Temple was badly damaged, almost destroyed.

The Sikhs never forgave Indira Gandhi. Protests in the form of marches were common, but hatred went deeper than that. In the eyes of most Sikhs, Mrs Gandhi had desecrated the Golden Temple and death threats became common. Sometimes there were as many as two or three a day. Mrs Gandhi took to wearing a bulletproof waistcoat, a sensible precaution given the waves of hate emanating from the Sikhs in the Punjab and across India.

On the morning of 31 October 1984, Indira Gandhi left her house, walking the short distance to her office. She was on her way to a meeting with British actor and broadcaster Peter Ustinov, who was intending to interview her for a television show. He was waiting with his film crew when he heard three loud bangs from the walkway outside:

'I heard three single shots. We looked alarmed but the people in the office said it must be firecrackers. Then there was a burst of automatic fire … We saw soldiers running. They kept us there for five hours. It became like a prison.'[3]

What Ustinov heard were the sounds of an assassination, the killing of Prime Minister Indira Gandhi. Surprisingly, Mrs Gandhi had retained a number of Sikhs in her bodyguard, insisting that retention of the men would show tolerance and good faith on her part. That day, she also decided not to wear her bulletproof jacket as it would bulge out and appear incongruous under her sari.

It was just before 9.15 pm when two of her Sikh guards turned on Indira Gandhi and shot her. Sub-Inspector Beant Singh fired first, putting three rounds from his revolver into her body. As she fell to the ground, his fellow assassin, Satwant Singh, opened fire with a sub-machine gun. Thirty rounds were fired at the dying Indira Gandhi.

At first, neither assassin tried to flee. Death and martyrdom awaited them and they simply dropped their weapons and stood waiting. The two bodyguards were captured by commandoes from the Indian-Tibetan police who made up the security on Mrs Gandhi's compound. Beaten and battered, they were taken to a security hut. At that point the assassins decided to make a run for it. Beant Singh was immediately shot dead, Satwant Singh wounded. He was later put on trial and executed in January of the following year.

Indira Gandhi was rushed to hospital. She was already dead when she arrived, but nevertheless it was felt to be politic to treat her as if she was still alive. Doctors operated on her and removed nearly twenty bullets from her body.

Blood transfusions were given and an appeal for more blood was made. It resulted in riots as members of the public fought and scrabbled in order to donate their blood. It was all part of a foolish and pointless charade, and at 4.30 pm Mrs Gandhi was pronounced dead.[4]

Following Indira Gandhi's death, there were anti-Sikh riots in northern India, resulting in many deaths and injuries. Sikh independence did not happen.

Rajiv Gandhi, Prime Minister of India (assassinated 21 May 1991)

Rajiv Gandhi, son of Indira and grandson of Jawaharlal Nehru, became Prime Minister of India when he succeeded his mother in 1984, serving until 1989 when he resigned. Previously never really interested in politics, Rajiv found himself 'forced' to become the leader of his family and of his country when Indira Gandhi was assassinated.

Disinterested as he was, Rajiv did help to 'pump prime' the Indian software industry, now a mainstay of the Indian economy, but he also made several grave mistakes during his period at the helm.

Chief amongst these errors was his decision to despatch the Indian Peace-Keeping Force to the independent state of Sri Lanka. Their aim was to assist the political leaders and government on the island in dealing with the rebel Tamil Tigers.

Rather like his mother's refusal to consider Sikh independence in the Punjab, Rajiv Gandhi's decision to oppose the Tamil Tigers' attempt at creating an independent Tamil state in Sri Lanka was to bring about his downfall and death.

On 21 May 1991, Rajiv was due to address a large crowd of supporters outside Madras during campaigning for parliamentary elections. He was walking through the dense crowd, heading towards the platform to begin his address, when a woman suddenly barred his path. She threw herself down before him, supposedly to kiss his feet. Immediately, a bomb concealed beneath her sari was exploded, killing both the assassin and Ranjit Gandhi. The assassin's head was apparently blown clean off.

Despite this, the assassin was never identified. The police suspected that the murder was the work of the Tamil Tigers but could find no evidence to prove it. Although the Tigers denied the accusation, the police maintained their belief and three months after the assassination produced evidence that it was the work of Raja Arumainayagam, head of intelligence for the Tamil Tigers.

Whoever organized the killing, it proved to be a pointless exercise. If anything, Ranjit Gandhi's death gave the Sri Lankan government extra determination. They eventually achieved victory over the Tamil Tigers in the early part of the twenty-first century.

Pablo Escobar, drug dealer and politician, Columbia (assassinated 2 December 1993)

Drug dealer, criminal gang boss and Columbian politician Pablo Escobar was, at one stage, amongst the richest men in the world, his fortune at the time of his death being estimated at US$ 30 billion. That would now be worth somewhere in the region of 70 billion.

Escobar began studying at university but dropped out and did not complete his course. Criminal activities were more appealing to him. He began in a small way, with automobile theft and selling fake lottery tickets. It was not long, however, before he became involved with drug smuggling and kidnapping, holding victims to ransom for what soon became large sums of money.

He had dreams of even bigger things, and in 1976 Escobar founded the Medellin Cartel. Under his sole leadership, the cartel created the first drug-smuggling route from Peru and other South American countries, through Colombia and the Bahamas, into the USA. It was a goldmine for Escobar. The more cocaine he could get into America, the more the demand for it grew.

As that demand increased, so did Escobar's power. By the 1980s, the Medellin Cartel was shipping many tons of the drug each year into the USA; nobody seemed able to stop them. Rival drug cartels were eliminated or controlled, with the 'King of Cocaine' happy to murder or assassinate policemen, judges, politicians and anyone else who challenged his position.

In the 1982 Colombian parliamentary elections, Pablo Escobar stood and was returned as a Liberal Party member of the Chamber of Representatives. He became responsible for a wide range of community projects, ranging from the creation of quality housing estates to sports facilities. His popularity with the Columbian people soared, and soon he was regarded as a South American Robin Hood.

It was something of a false dawn for the drug dealer as, despite his position as a popular politician, both the Columbian government and the USA were constantly pushing for his arrest. It did not stop Escobar's criminal activities – bombing, shooting and drug dealing continued as normal.

The pressure on Escobar was intense, however, and in 1991 he brokered a deal with the Colombian President. He would abandon his criminal activities and surrender, accepting a five-year prison sentence for his misdeeds. There was a catch to his offer. He would do all this provided he could spend his time in custody at his own purpose-built house/prison. La Cathedral, as it was known, was the height of luxury, with swimming pools, jacuzzis, football pitches and a well-equipped bar.

While for Escobar it was a good result, there were many who objected violently to his so-called imprisonment. He had already been expelled from the Liberal Party by its leader and presidential hopeful Luis Carlos Galan. Escobar responded to this insult by having Galan assassinated.

He went one stage further by planting a bomb on Avianca Flight 203, which was meant to be carrying Galan's successor. The new Liberal leader missed the plane and thus survived, but 107 other passengers did not.

When, in 1992, Escobar heard the news, via his unofficial grapevine, that he was about to be moved to a traditional Colombian prison, he contrived to escape. He spent the next fifteen months on the run. The Medellin Cartel crumbled and a nationwide manhunt kept Escobar in hiding, chased by the Columbian police and by Cali Cartel.

When he was finally run to earth at his house in Medellin, security forces funded and equipped by the USA surrounded the place and ordered him to surrender. He attempted to escape over the roof, but Escobar was shot in the body and the head. He died instantly. That suited the Columbian government perfectly – Pablo Escobar was never intended to survive the raid on his house.

Escobar's popularity did not die with him. More than 25,000 people attended his funeral and he was elevated to a position close to sainthood within Columbia. His personal estate was commandeered by the government and converted into a theme park. Even in death, it seemed, Pablo Escobar could do no wrong in the eyes of his supporters.

Andreas Escobar, footballer, Columbia (assassinated 2 July 1994)

Columbian soccer star Andreas Escobar was one of the first sportsmen or women to be assassinated as a direct result of the game they played. Nicknamed 'The Gentleman' because of his calmness and exemplary behaviour on the football field, he was assassinated in the aftermath of the 1994 World Cup.

Escobar was reviled by many Columbian supporters after scoring an own goal in the match against the USA. Columbia went on to lose the game 2–1 and were duly knocked out of the tournament. Angry fans derided Escobar's performance, claiming he had brought disgrace on the team and tarnished the image of his country. The criticism was unremitting and vicious.

For the star centre back, who had previously garnered only good reviews, it was hard to take. Nevertheless, he returned to Columbia with the rest of the squad and began to pick up the pieces of his career with Athletico Nacional. He was due to be transferred to Italian giants AC Milan and needed to put the American game behind him.

On the evening of 1 July 1994, Escobar called on a group of friends and they went to a bar before moving on to a club called El Indio in Santiago. During the evening, the friends split up, leaving Escobar alone in the car park at 3.00 am on the morning of 2 July.

A small group of men approached the footballer as he was standing by his car. An argument ensued, voices were raised and one of the men produced a .38 revolver. He shot Andreas Escobar six times, one of the other assailants apparently shouting 'Goal!' each time a bullet struck home. As Escobar fell, the assassins leapt into a pick-up truck and drove away. Their victim bled to death.

Police quickly arrested Humberto Castro Munoz, a bodyguard and driver for a Columbian drug cartel. He confessed to the killing, stating that his boss, cartel leader Santiago Gallon, had bet on Columbia to win the match against the USA and had lost heavily when they were defeated. That loss, he declared, was down to Escobar's own goal. On his own initiative, perhaps with a little 'pushing' by Gallon, Munoz decided to take his revenge.

Munoz was sentenced to forty-three years in prison, a term later reduced to twenty-six years. His accomplices were not identified, and the Gallon brothers, who ran the cartel, were not charged. There was no evidence against them apart from the statement by Munoz.

Most Columbians believed that the shooting was directly related to the game their country had lost. Former coach Francisco Marihuana, however, was clear that the assassination was a mistake. Escobar, he said, was simply in the wrong place at the wrong time and became a victim of the drug cartel. It remains hard to decide who was right, but 120,000 sports fans turned up at Escobar's funeral. They were there simply to mourn their hero.

Yitzhak Rabin, Prime Minister of Israel, Tel Aviv (assassinated 4 November 1995)

Yitzhak Rabin, when warned of an extremist Israeli plot to kill him, had once declared: 'I do not believe a Jew will kill a Jew.' His hopes and dreams for peace in Israel and Palestine had not been universally accepted, and despite his bold words he was in mortal danger.[5]

Like many other political leaders, Rabin was careless of his own safety; on 4 November 1995, his prediction was proved wrong. He was assassinated by Yigael Amir, a right-wing Jewish student and member of the extremist Eyal group.

A man of peace rather than war, Rabin served two terms as Prime Minister of Israel. Despite his personal stance, in 1976 he ordered the Israeli raid on Entebbe Airport to rescue Jewish hostages being held there by Palestinian terrorists. Peace, however, was constantly on his mind. He was actually speaking at a peace rally in Tel Aviv when he was shot and killed.

The previous months had seen increased anti-Rabin protests in Israel, much of it co-ordinated by future Prime Minister Benjamin Netanyahu. With marches where the crowd screamed 'Death to Rabin' and posters declaring him to be the new Adolf Hitler, the opponents to the ongoing Oslo Accords sought any chance to criticize Rabin.

The Accords were effectively peace negotiations between Israel and the Palestine Liberation Organization. They promoted recognition of each other by the two parties, the arrangements including Israel's withdrawal from the Gaza Strip. That was what really hurt the radical Israeli elements like Netanyahu's Likud Party, which was clear that any withdrawal from Jewish-held territory was tantamount to heresy and betrayal.

Yigal Amir, the assassin, held the view that he was merely obeying orders from God when he shot Yitzak Rabin with a Beretta semi-automatic pistol. His brother, Hagai, had assisted him by turning the revolver's bullets into dum-dum shells which would fragment and cause huge damage when they hit their target.

As the peace rally ended, Rabin walked down the steps of the town hall towards his car when Yigal Amir approached him from behind and fired two bullets into his back. Rabin's security guards instantly grabbed Amir, but not before he had fired another bullet into the arm of one of them.

Rabin was rushed to a nearby hospital, but the crowds in the streets delayed his arrival. It was ten minutes before he finally arrived, by which time his heart had stopped beating. Doctors managed to briefly resuscitate him, but the damage from the dum-dum bullets was too great and he was pronounced dead just after 11.00 pm.

In the wake of Rabin's death, hopes for a lasting peace in Palestine and Israel fell apart. The Oslo Accords stuttered to a conclusion, and from Yigal Amir's point of view the assassination was a successful enterprise. Without Yitzhak Rabin, there was simply no driving force from the Israeli side.

Condolences were sent from both sides of the conflict, and Hosni Mubarak, President of Egypt, even attended the funeral. Yasser Arafat of the PLO, it is said, made a secret visit to meet with Rabin's wife. As for the assassin, Yigal Amir's comment was simple: 'He deserved to die.' Amir was sentenced to life in prison.

Chapter Ten

Failed Assassination Attempts

The twentieth century might be full of successful assassinations that ended lives and destroyed government regimes, but it was also home to a whole host of failed killing attempts. Sometimes these failures were down to human error, sometimes part of abandoned schemes that were never implemented, ideas that never got beyond the planning stage. Either way, they are worth looking at.

Adolf Hitler, Fuhrer of Germany

Adolf Hitler is a good place to start. He escaped forty-two assassination attempts, mostly by a combination of good luck and the reckless behaviour of the plotters. As most people know, he finally committed suicide in April 1945 in the bunker below his bombed-out Reich Chancellery. There may well have been more attempts on his life, but the ones mentioned here are those that are best known.

The first recognized assassination plot took place just before Hitler became Chancellor in January 1933. One evening towards the end of the previous year, Hitler and a group of dignitaries dined at the exclusive Kaiserhof Hotel in Berlin. Afterwards, the whole party went down with sickness and diarrhoea.

It was not a case of food poisoning throughout the hotel's kitchens due to poor hygiene, as other guests who ate the same food were not ill. Although Hitler was less affected than the rest of his party, presumably due to his vegetarian diet, it was felt that somebody had deliberately poisoned the food. The guilty party, if there was one, was never discovered.

Beppo Roma, a former SA man, made two attempts to kill Hitler as revenge for the Night of the Long Knives that had claimed the lives of so many of his comrades. The first time, in 1934, his plot was discovered before it really got off the ground and Beppo was turned over to the Gestapo. He spent the next five years in Dachau Concentration Camp.

Released in 1939, he began his rediscovered freedom with tirades against the Nazi Party. He then began to plot again against Hitler, looking for the most effective way of despatching a man he saw as his chief enemy. Once again, his intentions were revealed, mainly because of his outspoken criticism of the Party and threats or promises regarding exactly what he was intending to do. Beppo was sent back to a concentration camp, where he was executed in 1944.

There were several other assassination plots against Hitler in the 1930s, but two stand out as 'near-run things'. Firstly, there was the attempt to blow him up during a parade to celebrate the German victory over Poland. It was 5 October 1939 and General Michal Karaszewicz-Tokarzewski laid explosive charges in a ditch alongside the road where the parade, with Hitler at its head, was to pass. Unfortunately, the parade was diverted and took another route, and the bomb went off harmlessly.

Then on 8 November 1939, Georg Elser planted a bomb in the Burgerbraukeller in Munich where Hitler was due to speak. Unfortunately for Elser, Hitler finished his speech early and left before the bomb went off. Eight spectators were killed and more than sixty wounded. Elser was arrested attempting to flee to Switzerland and sent to Dachau, where he was executed just a few days before the German surrender in 1945.

One very lucky failure came in March 1943 when three separate attempts to assassinate Hitler while he was flying back from the Eastern Front all failed. The most notable was a bomb which ground staff lodged in the aircraft's hold, where its timing mechanism froze and the explosive charge did not work. Once Hitler's plane landed in Berlin, the assassin managed to get to the bomb and disarm it before it exploded.

In 1944, the British Special Operations Executive (SOE) began formulating a series of plans known as Operation Foxley. These ranged from the simple idea of a sniper shooting Hitler while he was taking his morning walk to the derailment of his personal train. Loading his drinking water with a tasteless poison was probably one of the more realistic ideas that SOE came up with.

The most bizarre of the Operation Foxley plans was to hypnotize Rudolph Hess, who was then in captivity in Wales, and return him to Germany with instructions to kill Hitler.

None of the Operation Foxley plans came to anything, which, considering the lunacy of some suggestions, was probably a good thing. One of the reasons for not proceeding with Foxley was Hitler's physical and mental deterioration.

His drug addiction spiralled during the war years, with Dr Theodore Morel injecting and dosing him with more than thirty lethal substances each day. The advent of Parkinson's Disease was obvious to everyone. It was far better to have a disorganized, confused and unapproachable German leader than the incisive and dynamic personality that had begun the war.

The most famous of all the assassination attempts on Hitler's life was the Bomb Plot of 20 July 1944, when a group of his senior generals and other staff attempted to kill him at the Wolf's Lair, his East Prussia headquarters.

Colonel Claus von Stauffenberg, a war hero who had lost the sight from one eye, his complete right hand and several fingers of his left, was just one of many German Army officers who had become disenchanted with the Nazi regime and appalled by some of the massacres they had heard about. As Chief of Staff in the German Reserve Army, he had immediate and regular access to Hitler.

On 20 July 1944, Stauffenberg carried a bomb concealed in a briefcase into the briefing room at the Wolf's Lair. With the timer set for thirty minutes, Stauffenberg made an excuse to leave the meeting and drove away. As he went, a loud explosion and a tall cloud of smoke from the buildings behind him convinced Stauffenberg that Hitler must be dead. Operation Valkyrie, the plan to seize vital parts of Berlin – the telephone exchange, the railway station and the radio network – was then put into action.

Hitler was not dead, however. A table leg had shielded him from the worst of the blast and ensured that he escaped with nothing more serious than pierced eardrums and superficial burns. It has been suggested, but never proved, that an officer at the table moved Stauffenberg's briefcase out of the reach of his feet, not knowing that his desire for comfort would save Hitler's life. Four of the other officers in the briefing room were killed, however, and twenty injured. Hitler, it seemed, had a mercurial and magical hold on life.

In the repercussions that swiftly followed the attempt, the plotters were despatched with what appeared to be a delicious mood of hatred and revenge. Some, including Stauffenberg, were shot immediately. They were the lucky ones. Others were forced to endure prison and trials before the inevitable guilty verdict was passed. Their deaths came in the form of hanging by piano wire.

Nobody was exempt, even men like Field Marshal Rommel perishing (by enforced suicide) in the sweeping fury of Hitler's vengeance. In all, over 4,000 deaths were the result of the bomb plot, and Hitler lived for another nine months.

Six US Presidents

In addition to the four US Presidents who were killed by assassins, there were six others who narrowly escaped with their lives. These were Theodore Roosevelt, Franklin Delano Roosevelt, Harry Truman, Ronald Reagan, Gerald Ford and Richard Nixon.

On 14 October 1912, **Theodore 'Teddy' Roosevelt** was the victim of a single shot fired by former saloon owner John Schrank as he was getting into his car prior to giving a campaign speech, hoping for a third term in office. The assassination attempt happened outside a hotel in Milwaukee.

According to doctors, the fifty-page speech, folded up and stored in his coat pocket, helped save Roosevelt's life. The bullet was diverted in its track by the bulky paper and the president's metal spectacle case. The bullet was never removed from his body.

Despite the pain and the blood that was pouring from the wound, Roosevelt refused to be taken to hospital, insisting that he be driven to the venue for his speech. He spoke for nearly an hour:

'Friends, I shall have to ask you to be as quiet as possible. I do not know if you fully understand that I have just been shot … The bullet is in me now, so that I cannot make a very long speech but I will try my best.'[1]

Schrank was found to be mentally deranged and sent to a psychiatric hospital, where he died in 1943. Teddy Roosevelt did not obtain the nomination, but he did split the Republican vote, leaving the coast clear for Democrat Woodrow Wilson.

Franklin Delano Roosevelt was president-elect when he was nearly assassinated by Italian Giuseppe Zangara on 15 February 1933. The motive for the attack is hard to define, as Zangara seemed to have no political axe to grind but did have a passionate hatred for rich capitalists.

Roosevelt had just spent a few days on a yacht off the coast of Florida. When he came ashore, he gave a brief speech at Bay Front Park in Miami. Zangara suddenly appeared and fired five shots at the would-be president. All of them missed their mark, although one hit Mayor Anton Cermak and four other people in the crowd. Cermak died a fortnight later.

Zangara, clearly insane, protested when he was given four twenty-year sentences, calling the judge 'tight' and daring him to sentence him to a longer period in jail. He got his wish, partially at least. When Mayor Cermak died, Zangara was brought back to court and sentenced to death. FDR went on to become the highly successful thirty-second President of the USA.

Roosevelt's successor as president, **Harry S Truman**, was yet another potential victim of assassins. Living in Blair House on Pennsylvania Avenue while the White House underwent repairs, Truman was attacked outside his house by Griselio Torresola and Oscar Collazo on the afternoon of 1 November 1950.

Both assassins were members of the Puerto Rican Nationalist Party, believing that the USA was responsible for the exploitation and oppression of Puerto Rican citizens, both in America and Puerto Rico. The death of Truman, they believed, would start a revolution in the USA, one of the results being a return of freedom and independence to Puerto Rico.

The assassination attempt was bungled and inept. The assassins arrived outside Blair House and began shooting wildly and inaccurately at the building. Although Truman was inside and did view things from an upstairs window, he was never in serious danger. Two security men were wounded, an army soldier killed and assassin Torresola shot in the head. He died instantly, while Collazo was wounded and sentenced to life imprisonment. He was released in 1979 and returned to Puerto Rico.

Richard Nixon was nothing if not a controversial figure. Famous for his television debates with JFK and in particular for the Watergate Affair, he was also a target for assassination.

Samuel Joseph Byck, a tyre salesman and something of a bizarre character, hated Nixon and all that he stood for. He was a manic depressive who blamed Nixon for his failure to be given a business loan. Matters came to a head on 22 February 1974 when, unable to take any more failure and disappointment, Byck drove to Baltimore-Washington Airport armed with a pistol and a gasoline bomb.

His plan was simple: he would commandeer an aircraft and force the pilot to crash it into the White House. That, Byck believed, would take care of Nixon and various members of his staff. From the beginning, however, his scheme dissolved into violence.

Upon arrival at the airport, Byck immediately shot one of the security guards and then, as chaos and confusion reigned, forced his way onto Delta Flight 523. He burst into the cockpit and shot and killed the co-pilot. Waving his pistol under the pilot's nose, Byck ordered the man to take off. Bravely, the pilot refused. Byck's response was to grab a female passenger, drag her into the cockpit and order her to help the pilot to fly the aircraft. Quite how she was supposed to do this was never made clear.

By now, security units had surrounded the plane and began firing at the cockpit. It was a 'gung-ho' approach to the problem, but Byck had a gun and had already used it. Bullet after bullet smashed into the aircraft, Byck being hit in the chest and stomach. In obvious agony, he turned his gun on himself. He shot himself in the head and died in the plane cockpit.

Richard Nixon was never in any danger, but Byck's deranged assassination attempt has to be one of the strangest of all attempts to kill a US President. A few days before the incident, he had sent a tape recording detailing his plan to the press. It was the first occasion anyone had thought of crashing an aeroplane into a designated terrorist target – as we know, it would not be the last.

President Gerald Ford was on his way to deliver a speech on crime when he was attacked by Lynette 'Squeaky' Fromme, one of the fanatical supporters and followers of Sharon Tate killer Charles Manson. It was Friday, 5 September 1975. Ford was walking, shaking hands with passers-by, covering the short distance between his hotel and the Capital Building in Sacramento, California.

The gun used by 'Squeaky' Fromme had bullets in the weapons clip but none in the chamber. As soon as he saw Fromme pull out the gun, aim at the president and pull the trigger, a security man pushed his finger in front of the firing pin and grabbed her, thereby preventing a second attempt. Fromme was immediately arrested and later sentenced to life in prison.

Fromme's motive was simple. She wanted to draw attention to what she believed was the unjust imprisonment of Manson, who would be called as a witness and tell the world about his beliefs.

A second attempt on the life of Gerald Ford took place a few weeks later, on22 September. The failed assassin this time was Sara Jane Moore, who was trying to re-establish links with left-wing groups. Unsuccessful in the assassination attempt, she was sentenced to life in prison. Ford must have wondered what he had done wrong.

Ronald Reagan was badly wounded in an assassination attempt on 30 March 1980. His attacker was John Hinckley, an unbalanced young man with an obsession for actress Jodie Foster. Hinckley believed that by killing President Reagan, he would impress Jodie with what he described as 'the greatest offering of love in the world'.

Reagan was shot outside the Hilton Hotel in Washington DC, a single bullet ricocheting off his car and entering his body under the left armpit. It eventually lodged in his lung, leaving him closer to death than anyone ever imagined. Three other members of the president's entourage were shot and wounded in the volley of bullets.

Reagan survived, but took several months to recover. His ready wit – he apparently told his wife that he was wounded simply because he had forgotten to duck and joked with his doctors, before going under the anaesthetic, about their political affinity – disappeared. Humour was one thing; he was lucky to survive the ordeal.

Hinckley was sentenced to a period of indefinite confinement in a Washington psychiatric hospital. A letter he had written to Jodie Foster just a few hours before the assassination attempt gave a clear indication of his intent, his obvious emotional disturbance and his fascination with the actress:

'Jodie, I would abandon this idea of getting Reagan in a second if I could only win your heart and live out the rest of my life with you, whether it be in total obscurity or whatever.'[2]

As Foster later acknowledged, Hinckley had confused love with obsession. He also had a desire to be famous. That, at least, was something he achieved.

*   *   *

Failed assassination attempts were as common in the final part of the twentieth century as they were at the beginning. Many of them were organized and put into operation by various state governments, others by unhappy and disturbed individuals. The one thing they all had in common was that they failed.

Lenin and Stalin

In any study of the Russian Revolution, in-depth or brief, Vladimir Lenin is invariably compared to Joseph Stalin. The butcher Stalin comes out as the personification of evil; Lenin, on the other hand, is usually thought of as a compassionate revolutionary who always had the good of his people at heart. Both views are somewhat simplistic; Stalin less so than Lenin.

Lenin was not the idyllic and pacific leader he is still often considered to have been. As the chief architect of the Bolshevik revolution and as the first Premier of communist Russia, he was ruthless, determined and unrelenting in his views. He had to be. Consequently, he garnered enemies from all corners of the Russian Empire, although perhaps not as many as his predecessor, Czar Nicholas II, or his successor, Stalin. Even so, they were there, awaiting an opportunity and not frightened to act.

On 30 August 1918, Lenin gave an address to the workers at the Michelson Factory in Moscow. Following his speech, he left the factory, pushing his way through the crowd of admirers that had gathered. He was approached by Fanya Kaplan, who immediately pulled out a pistol and fired three shots at him. The first passed harmlessly through his coat, but the second and third hit him in the left arm and, most significantly, smashed into his left lung and lodged close to the collarbone.

Lenin refused to go to hospital, fearing that other assassins would be waiting, and was driven to the Kremlin. Once there, the seriousness of the wounds was realized. He had the strength to walk upstairs to his bedroom, but by the time he reached it he was in agony. Doctors were called, but without specialized surgery they were reluctant to attempt removing the two bullets.

Amazingly, thanks to his superb self-control and strength, Lenin recovered and the bullets were never removed. Fanya Kaplan, a member of an anti-Stalin group of revolutionaries, had a history of violence. She had spent years in prison for the attempting shooting of a czarist official and had only recently been released.

Detained after the shooting, Kaplan refused to co-operate and was clearly insane. She was taken to a cellar in the Kremlin and killed by a single shot into the back of the head.

Lenin might have recovered, but his health was seriously impaired. Four years after the assassination attempt, he began to experience seizures as a result of lead poisoning, possibly caused by the two bullets still lodged in his body. He became increasingly unwell, suffering a stroke in March 1923 which took away his power of speech. Another stroke, in January 1924, finally killed him.

After much confusion and in-fighting, Joseph Stalin succeeded Lenin as leader of the USSR. As his period in power became increasingly intolerant and tyrannical, Stalin was subjected to a number of assassination attempts. For a variety of reasons, they all failed or were abandoned.

Operation Long Jump was a convoluted plot concocted by the Nazis' Third Reich, which was intended to be led by Obersturmbannfuhrer Otto Skorzeny. The Big Three – Stalin, Churchill and FDR – were to be assassinated simultaneously while attending the Tehran Conference in 1943. The plot was uncovered by a Russian spy and the whole affair was abandoned. A similar plot, Operation Zeppelin, with the aim of poisoning Stalin, was aborted at the same time.

Perhaps the most dangerous plot was the one designed by former KGB Chief G.S. Luzhkov, who had deserted to Japan in 1938. He came up with a plan to kill Stalin while he was bathing in the hot springs at Matsesta on the Black Sea coast. Unfortunately, the assassination team was spotted while crossing the border, three of the six men being instantly killed.[3]

Cold War Targets

Marshal Tito, real name Josip Broz, was a war hero, a resistance fighter in the Balkans during the Second World War. In the wake of the Nazi defeat, he united the various Balkan states into the communist power of Yugoslavia.

Never a hardliner, Tito created a brand of socialism known as Titoism and soon antagonized Stalin, so much so that the Russian leader sent various agents to assassinate him. None of them were successful, but they annoyed Tito so much that he wrote a letter of protest to the Russian leader, a missive later found in his desk after Stalin's death:

'Stop sending people to murder me. We have captured five of them, one with a bomb and another with a rifle. If you don't stop sending killers I will send one to Moscow, and there'll be no need to send any more.'[4]

Stalin, however, was determined to end Tito's reign and life. He despatched Josif Grigulevich, an experienced diplomat and assassin, to familiarize himself with Tito and the country. Grigulevich even met Tito himself.

He returned to Moscow and sent his plan for the assassination of Tito to Stalin. It was 1 March 1953, and the following day Stalin suffered a stroke. It is doubtful if Stalin ever read the plan. He died three days later, and the project to assassinate Marshal Tito was dropped.

Alexander Solzhenitsyn was perhaps the greatest writer to come out of Russia since Tolstoy. With books like *The Gulag Archipelago* and *Cancer Ward* to his name, he won the Nobel Prize for Literature, but in so doing further antagonized the Russian government and its KGB agents.

Solzhenitsyn had spent eight years in Russian prisons, being released in 1953, only to face a further three years of exile. In 1962, during a de-Stalinization period in Russia, he *wrote A Day in the Life of Ivan Denisovich*, which was hugely critical of the Gulag system. It was published without any form of censorship. Further critical works, however, brought him only grief, with a ban on any of his work being published in Russia.

Several novels were published outside Russia, the Nobel Prize coming in 1970. Solzhenitsyn did not attend the ceremony in Sweden, afraid he would not be allowed back into Russia. At that point, the KGB decided to take action. His books, it was felt, were tantamount to treason.

Solzhenitsyn was standing at the counter in a store in Rostov-on-Don when a KGB agent came up behind him and stabbed him with a poisoned needle. Solzhenitsyn did not feel the prick of the needle going in. The assassination attempt failed to kill him, the poison having not worked, and for many years he did not even know he had been attacked, not even when his body later burst out in dreadful sores and burns. Solzhenitsyn only learned of the attack in 1992 when it was revealed in a Russian newspaper article.

A few years after the assassination attempt, the Russian government exiled Solzhenitsyn. He went to live in the USA, where he remained until 1994 when the new regime of Mikhail Gorbachev restored his Russian citizenship, dropped treason charges and allowed him back to Moscow. He died peacefully at the age of 89.

Fidel Castro was, in the 1960s, felt by the Americas to be the chief proponent of anti-US feelings and fears. It was thus not long before he became the chief target for the security agencies of the US government.

When he came to power in Cuba at the end of 1959, Castro's revolution sent warning flags shooting to the top of the US flagpole. A revolutionary leader who was based just 90 miles away from Florida was something that did not sit easily with the Americans.

Castro had not yet proclaimed himself a communist, but the adoption of such a stance was always a distinct possibility. Two years later, when Castro welcomed the placement of Nikita Khrushchev's nuclear missiles on the island, the world came closer to nuclear war than it ever had been.

President Kennedy and his advisors fashioned a retaliation of sorts, creating a quarantine line over which Soviet ships could not pass. A game of bluff and counter-bluff between Khrushchev and the American president began. Ultimately, with honours even, the Russian missiles were withdrawn, as were American rockets in Turkey. Nevertheless, the looming figure of Castro remained in power.

There had been attempts to assassinate Castro for several years, popular estimates stating that there were well over 600 plots or plans to end his life. Most of these were CIA-funded or led and most of them were simply out of this world. Luckily, the foolish options, better suited to children's comic books or television cartoon shows, never became reality. The main concern lies in the simple fact that they were even mooted in the first place.

Early assassination attempts included a plan to spray the room where Castro was broadcasting to his supporters with a chemical compound, comparable to LSD. Castro would, the CIA believed, become confused, literally 'spaced out'. That would serve only to ridicule the Cuban leader in the eyes of the people he was addressing. The plan was dropped before it could fail.

One of the best-known schemes was connected to Castro's love of diving. It was suggested that Castro's wetsuit could be coated with an infectious poison that would, over a long period of time, kill him.

Again, the idea was shelved. Poison in his food and cigars coated with toxins were next on the agenda. They were also abandoned for want of a suitable agent to actually plant the poisoned articles.

And so it went on until, in 1961, John F. Kennedy passed the assassination task to his brother, Bobby, the US Attorney General. Both Kennedys were clear that Fidel Castro was a serious threat to world peace and needed to be removed. For 'removed', read 'assassinated'.

Entitled Operation Mongoose, the plans that emerged from the change of focus were as silly and pathetic as the previous CIA efforts. They were mostly not shared with the American public at the time; to have done so would surely have ruined the Kennedy ideal of a new Camelot. But after JFK's own assassination, the inane and ludicrous plots gradually became common knowledge. Some US citizens rejected the whole concept of the 'Assassinate Castro' notion, but others accepted it as fact.

Operation Mongoose began with the ludicrous notion of painting Castro's shoes with poisonous chemicals. Over a period of time, Castro's beard would fall out, humiliating him before his followers and destroying his most notable feature.

Then there was the plan to lure Castro to Finca Vigia, the farmhouse that had once belonged to Ernest Hemingway and was now in the process of being presented to the Cuban government for conversion to a museum. Hemingway's fourth wife had met with Castro and even shown him around the place. The Cuban leader was a great fan of Hemingway and it was felt he would not be able to refuse another invitation to the farm. Once Castro was inside the house, a CIA bomb would blow up both the house and the Cuban leader.

Neither plan came to fruition, and when rumours began to spread, American politicians were quick to distance themselves from the various schemes. Robert McNamara, Kennedy's Defence Secretary, when questioned about the proposed bombing of Finca Vigia, was one of the first to deny knowledge of it and of any other assassination attempts:

'I don't know anything about it. The whole Operation Mongoose thing was insane.'[5]

He was certainly right about the insanity of it all. Other ridiculous notions included the planting of an exploding conch shell at Castro's favourite diving spot. Contact was even made with senior officers in the Mafia, who would be paid handsomely for an Underworld-style 'hit' on Castro.

One of the final plots hatched during Bobby Kennedy's tenure as Attorney General was perhaps the most stupid of them all. The plan called for two US submarines to lie submerged off Havana. As dawn broke, they would surface and fire star shells over the town. The religious and superstitious Cubans would think it was the second coming of Christ and would promptly overthrow Castro's regime.[6]

The 'adolescent' responses of the CIA – and, for that matter, of the two Kennedys – were perhaps symptomatic of the times. Knee-jerk reactions were the order of the day, featuring in many of America's policy decisions.

As for the bizarre nature of the proposed assassinations, it was hardly surprising when you consider that JFK's favourite reading material was the James Bond stories of Ian Fleming.

General Charles De Gaulle became President of France in 1959, having risen to fame as the leader of the Free French movement during the Second World War.

To the end of his life, he was a staunch anti-communist. He was also committed to the process of granting independence and releasing French colonies across the world. That set him up perfectly for a number of assassination attempts by the OAS, the secret military organization determined to hold onto French territories.

It is estimated that there were at least thirty attempts on De Gaulle's life, most of them during his ten years as president. Not all of the assassination attempts were by the OAS; it even appears the CIA tried to kill him after he expelled American troops from France.

None of the attempts were successful, but some came very close. Many of them involved ambushing De Gaulle in his car. Perhaps the closest to success was an ambush on 22 August 1962, when De Gaulle and his wife were on their way to the airport. Fifteen OAS men attacked them in a Paris suburb, with more than 100 rounds of automatic fire aimed at the presidential car, twelve of them smashing their way into the vehicle, others hitting the tyres. De Gaulle was not hurt in the attack, but he did apparently cut his finger on a piece of broken glass as he brushed it off his clothes.

In August 1944, the president was attacked on his way into Notre Dame Cathedral. He could have dived for cover, but instead stood up at his full height and continued into the church to sing the Te Deum. Whatever else you might say about Charles De Gaulle, you could not doubt his bravery.

Andy Warhol, was eccentric, gifted and in his own way as significant as the surrealist painters of the Twenties and Thirties. Above all, he was a man who died twice! There are those who might say: 'Well, he would, wouldn't he?'

Artist, film-maker and popular icon, Warhol's first 'death' was a classic case of a man who found himself in the wrong place at the wrong time when he encountered a deranged and deadly woman who had nothing against him personally. Warhol was simply a representative of the one type of person his would-be assassin hated – he was a man.

On the evening of 3 June 1968, Warhol and his friend Jed Johnson arrived at The Factory, Warhol's studio in New York. Standing outside the building, as if she was waiting for them, was Valerie Solanas.

Solanas was an actor; perhaps not a very successful one, but she knew the film-maker quite well, and neither he nor Johnson showed any surprise at seeing her there. They did note that she was a lot tidier than normal. She wore makeup and her hair was combed and in place. That was unusual for a woman who had rejected all the normal standards of female behaviour and appearance.

Solanas had appeared in Warhol's film *I, a Man*, and to him and Johnson she was no more than an ambitious woman looking for her next role. They did not speak to her in great depth, but moved on into the building. Solanas followed them.

Once inside the studio, however, the behaviour of Solanas became increasingly odd. She literally bounced around on her feet as if she could not contain her excitement, and seemed unable to settle. She wore heavy clothes, despite the weather being hot, and kept a firm hold on a paper bag. After a few minutes, 'odd' changed to 'deadly'.

Solanas suddenly pulled a revolver out of the bag and began to shoot indiscriminately. Warhol was hit just once, the rest of the bullets striking two other men, Fred Hughes and Matio Amaya, who were working in the office. Then, as people dived for cover, her gun jammed and she ran out of the building.

Andy Warhol lay under his desk in a pool of blood. The bullet had gone through his right lung, his gall bladder, liver and intestines. It was, potentially, a fatal wound. It took half an hour to get him to hospital, and after some considerable time on the operating table Warhol was pronounced clinically dead.

Doctors were not willing to give up on him, however, and after a minute and a half of desperate effort, they managed to get his heart beating again. It took them nearly six hours to repair the damage from the gunshot, and Warhol was in hospital for a month. In all, his recovery took over a year. Not bad for a man who was once dead.

Valerie Solanas turned herself in soon after the shooting, approaching and alarming a policeman in Times Square, then admitted her guilt.

Arrested, she was detained and taken into custody. To begin with, however, the police did not know if Warhol was dead or alive, so there was no official charge until the next morning, when the victim was declared to be still alive. The following day, as her lack of cooperation and deranged personality became obvious, she was committed to a mental hospital.

Two years earlier, in a self-published book entitled *The SCUM Manifesto*, Valerie Solinas had already declared her position:

'The male is an incomplete female, a walking abortion … To be male is to be deficient, emotionally limited; maleness is a deficiency disease and males are emotional cripples.'[7]

A verdict of mental incapacity was inevitable. She was released some years later and died from lung disease in a shelter for the homeless in 1988.

As for Andy Warhol, he continued to produce art, although many critics say that it was never as good or as striking as before the attempted assassination. In 1987, one year before Valerie Solinas, Warhol died for a second time, this time permanently from a heart attack.

Margaret Thatcher, Britain's first ever female prime minister, was the target for IRA bombers in October 1984. The assassination failed, but it proved that nobody was safe during the wave of terrorist bombings.

The unsuccessful attack came in the midst of the IRA bombing campaign and followed in the wake of the more successful bomb attacks on Lord Mountbatten and Airey Neave. In Thatcher's case, the bomb attack was more frightening – for her at least – than harmful, but the shockwaves from an attack on the PM reverberated around the globe.

There had only ever been one assassination of a British prime minister, that of Spencer Percival in 1812, although Queen Victoria had been subjected to numerous attacks during her reign. Politicians such as Robert Peel had also survived assassination attempts, so in the wake of the recent Mountbatten and Neave deaths, any assault – successful or otherwise – on a government figure was bound to be front-page news.

The bomb was planted on the sixth floor of the Grand Hotel in Brighton during the 1984 Conservative Party Conference. The assassin was Patrick Magee, who rented the room and took several weeks to knock down the wall in his bathroom. He managed to keep hotel staff away from his partially demolished bathroom and installed a gelignite bomb in the cavity. He then rebuilt the wall. Just before 3.00 am on 12 October, his bomb exploded.

The explosion caused the five floors between Patrick Magee's room and Margaret Thatcher's bathroom to collapse. The falling masonry should have killed her outright, but Thatcher had been delayed with party political business and was not in her bathroom.

She escaped uninjured, stoic and seemingly unshaken. Unfortunately, five of her colleagues were killed in the blast and two others seriously hurt.

Thatcher, renowned for her abrasive qualities, gave a speech to the Tory Conference just one day after the attempted assassination. She had to rewrite one or two passages of the speech, but seemed otherwise untroubled.

The police hunt for the assassin was intense and thorough. All of the hotel guests for the previous month were logged and, if possible, examined. There was only one visitor, a Roy Walsh, who could not be traced. Fingerprints from The Grand's registration books revealed him to actually be Patrick Magee, a renowned IRA terrorist. Magee was tracked down, arrested and sent for trial. He was given eight life sentences, but was later released after serving just fourteen years as part of the Good Friday Agreement that brought an end to the Troubles in Northern Ireland.

In hindsight, the poor security arrangements for Margaret Thatcher seem almost ludicrous. For an assassin to spend weeks breaking down walls in his bedroom, directly above the room where the Prime Minister of Great Britain was to stay, seems more the work of fiction than reality. It would probably be fair to say that such an attack would not be possible today.

Margaret Thatcher, a fighter and battler if nothing else, continued as prime minister with the avowed intention of defeating the IRA. They could not be allowed to win, she declared. Her reputation as an unmoveable force simply grew in strength.

Thatcher resigned in 1990, succeeded by John Major. She became a member of the House of Lords, and died in April 2013.

Epitaph/End Piece

It might be stating the obvious, but assassination did not stop at the end of the twentieth century. Political killing went on, continuing to shock and frighten members of the public as well as anyone in the public eye. There was a change to the process, however.

As the new century unfolded, assassinations increasingly became group operations. The day of the lone assassin was not exactly over, but with more and more governments and terrorist organizations acknowledging and using assassination as a weapon of war, it became more effective and more 'headline-grabbing' to take out twenty, hundreds, perhaps even thousands of opposition figures than one single individual.

The involvement and possible death of unknowing, uninvolved people in the activities of the victim was considered irrelevant. It was perhaps regrettable to the perpetrators, but not to the extent that they would stop a major plot or assassination attempt. The deaths of innocent bystanders could be called collateral damage, and such attacks have been increasingly seen as effective ways of getting to the point of the exercise.

The 9/11 attack on the Twin Towers in New York is a classic example, with thousands perishing in just a few minutes. It was the number of deaths that shocked people, not the identity of the victims. The Americans took their revenge with an attack by Navy Seals on the Pakistan compound of Osama bin Laden, and later on his son, Hamza bin Laden. In both assassinations, the Seals shot on sight, killing others apart from their main target.

The success or failure of assassination has always been a debatable point. Looking back over the cases mentioned in this book, only a handful of them achieved their desired aim; most simply hardened the viewpoint and opinions of the victim's supporters.

Whichever way you look at it, assassination is unpredictable. The only thing that is guaranteed is the determination and the desire of the perpetrators to carry out their task.

The situation is likely to change again, with the increasing use of drones in a military capacity rather than as observation devices taking much of the risk out of assassination. The use of drones is also likely to alter the attitude of observers and the watching or reading public. Drones equate with distance and take out the human or personal element. When you consider it, the personal touch is what makes TV documentaries about murderers and the like so popular. It is the same with assassination; that personal touch holding you to the subject.

There is little personality in a drone. The assassins of the next hundred years are therefore even less likely to succeed in their aim than the old-fashioned hit man or assassination team.

The settling of personal scores will continue, and for such assassinations there can be no modern, technological advances – in theory at least. The knife, the bullet, poison or explosives will probably remain the main tool.

*   *   *

I am conscious that in this book I have concerned myself with just over fifty assassination victims, along with perhaps fifteen or so fortunate escapees. When added up, it makes approximately seventy assassination attempts, all described in some detail, plus seven group assassinations such as the St Valentine's Day Massacre, the activities of the Cairo Gang in Ireland and little-known events like the Bloody Night in Portugal.

Seventy or so assassinations are not a huge total. There are hundreds more that are waiting to be taken up and described. That's a job for someone else at some time in the future.

While many assassinations were fairly routine, others that I came across were bizarre, either in the way the assassins operated or the type or style of death handed out to their victims. The various schemes to rid the world of Fidel Castro are worthy of any James Bond story, ranging from exploding cigars to poisonous shoes that would make his beard fall out.

Assassins' weapons ranged across the spectrum, from poison and knives to revolvers and sharpshooters' rifles. Interestingly, as writer Robert Baer has commented, the instruments of death were often cheap to buy, and that had grave consequences (no pun intended):

'The most iconic assassinations in history have been spare, economical acts … A psychotic Lee Harvey Oswald murdered Kennedy with a $10.95 mail order rifle. If nothing else he demonstrated that changing history is within anyone's reach.'[1]

Some of the assassins, men like Lee Harvey Oswald, themselves became victims of assassination. That was, in some respects, simply the name of the game; assassins could not hope for a nobler or quicker ending to their enterprises.

Then there are the peripheral players. There were dozens of them – men and women not directly concerned with assassination but who, in some minor way, contributed to the legends. Honourable mentions are here given to several people, including George Harrison and John Wayne. They do not feature heavily in the text, but they could have done. And there are so many more.

It would have been easy to research and write about those who have been omitted. Several writers have already done that, but it would have doubled, even trebled, the size of this book, and I wanted to keep it readable, not make a vast tome of facts and figures.

History is not a list of dates or names of battles, nor is it a glossary of kings and queens. History is about stories. Enjoying them, no matter what the subject matter, is the important factor. That is how we learn. And with learning we can hope not to repeat the same old mistakes, time after time. That, at least, is the theory.

The assassinations described here all contain what I call 'interesting facts'. That is why I chose them rather than other significant events and individuals that have been left out. I can only say that you should go away and research any twentieth-century assassinations that appeal to your imagination and interest. They may be very different from my choices. It is a fascinating topic and you will not have wasted your time.

Notes

Chapter One

1. Robert Baer, *The Perfect Kill* (W&N), p.XXI.
2. Jonathan Powell, article 'Why Assassination Doesn't Work', *The New Statesman* (30 June 2021).
3. Kenneth Baker, On Assassination (Unicorn), p.16.
4. https://ultimateclassicalrock.com/george/harrison.
5. Stephen Spignesi, *In the Crosshairs* (Skyhorse Publishing), p.263.
6. *Ibid.*, p.XVIII.
7. Caroline Moorhead, article 'Who Killed Daphne', *The Literary Review* (23 December 2003–24 January 2004), p.51.

Chapter Two

1. https://en.wikipedia.org/wiki/Gaetano-Bresci
2. Kenneth Baker, *ibid.*, p.177.
3. Evan Andrews, 'The Assassination of a President', www.//https/history.com.
4. Richard Cavendish, article 'The Strange Death of Emile Zola', *History Today* (Sept 2002).
5. Father Gapon, 'The Story of My Life', in *The Faber Book of Reportage* (Faber), p.415.
6. https://en.wikipedia.org/wiki/Bloody-Sunday-(1905).
7. Kenneth Baker, *ibid.*, p.147.
8. *Ibid.*, p.149.
9. *Ibid.*, p.146.
10. A.J.P. Taylor, *The First World War* (Penguin).
11. Borijove Jevtic, 'The Murder of the Archduke Franz Ferdinand',' in *The Faber Book of Reportage*, p.443.
12. Borijove Jevtic, *ibid.*, p.443.

Chapter Three

1. Stephen Spignesi, *In the Crosshairs*, p.243.
2. *Ibid.*, p.214.
3. Phil Carradice, *A Hundred Years of Spying* (Pen & Sword), p.56.
4. https://en.wikipedia.org/wiki/Mata-Hari.

5. Robert Massie, *Nicholas and Alexandra* (Random House), p.134.
6. https://www.bing.com/search?+czar-Nicholas.
7. https://enwikipedia.org/wiki-Karl-Leibnacht.
8. Quoted in https://www.bing.com/search-rosa.luxenberg.

Chapter Four

1. https://en.wikipedia.org/wiki/Cairo-Gang.
2. *Ibid.*
3. Kenneth Baker, *ibid.*, p.52.

Chapter Five

1. Phil Carradice, *The Night of the Long Knives* (Pen & Sword), p.78.
2. *Ibid.*, p.13.
3. Article, *Time Magazine* (1934).
4. Phil Carradice, *The Night of the Long Knives*, p.95.

Chapter Six

1. www.//histrory.com/this-day-in-history/stalin-banished-trotsky.
2. Ramon Mercader, quoted in *In the Crosshairs* by Stephen Spignesi, pp.293–294.
3. Quoted in https://bing/search-heydrich-reinhart.
4. Article 'The twilight of Italian Fascism, *Enter, Stage Right* (2008).
5. John Withington, *Assassins' Deeds* (Reaktion Books), p.219.
6. Stephen Spignesi, *In the Crosshairs*, p.93.

Chapter Seven

1. Kenneth Baker, *ibid.*, p.206.
2. John Withington, *ibid.*, p.245.
3. Stephen Spignesi, *ibid.*, p.153.
4. Article in *The New York Times* (27 November 1963), p.A1.
5. Article in *The New York Times* (2 December 1963), p.121.
6. www://thenation.com/article/archives/hendrik-verewoerd.

Chapter Eight

1. https://wikipedia.org/wiki/Vivtor-Jara.
2. Article in *The Guardian* (14 September 1977).
3. Kenneth Baker, *ibid.*, p.228.

Chapter Nine

1. *Times Union* (29 August 2012), quoted in https://en.wikipedia.org/Murder-of-John-Lennon.
2. *Times Union* (21 August 2012).
3. Anon., *Indira Gandhi, Personal and Political Biography*, p.17.

4. Kenneth Baker, *ibid.*, p.214.
5. Quoted in *In the Crosshairs* by Stephen Spignesi, p.237.

Chapter Ten
1. Quoted in *In the Crosshairs*, p.259.
2. Letter to Jodie Foster, Public Domain, see *In the Crosshairs*, p.249.
3. https://historystockexchange.com.
4. https://sinple.wikipedia.org/wiki/Josip-Broz-Tito.
5. https://www.thenation.com/article/archive/CIA-kennedplot-kill-Castro.
6. Phil Carradice, *The Cuban Missile Crisis* (Pen & Sword), pp.24–25.
7. Valeria Solinas, *The SCUM Manifesto* (self-published).

Epitaph
1. Robert Baer, *The Perfect Kill*, p.51.

Bibliography

Primary Sources
Jevtic, Borijove, 'The Murder of Archduke Ferdinand', published in *New York World* (29 June 1924) – first-hand account by one of the assassins.
Hindley, John, letter to Jodie Foster, written March 1981 – in Public Domain.
Solinas, Valeria, *The SCUM Manifesto* (self-published, 1966).

Books
Baer, Robert, *The Perfect Kill* (London: Weidenfeld & Nicolson, 2015).
Baker, Kenneth, *On Assassinations* (London: Unicorn, 2020).
Carey, John (ed.), *The Faber Book of Reportage* (London: Faber, 1987).
Carradice, Phil, *A Hundred Years of Spying* (Barnsley: Pen & Sword, 2021).
Carradice, Phil, *The Cuban Missile Crisis* (Barnsley: Pen & Sword, 2017).
Carradice, Phil, *The Night of the Long Knives* (Barnsley: Pen & Sword, 2020).
Cocks, Chris, *Deslocado Redemption* (self-published, 2018).
Colville, John, *The Fringes of Power* (London: Hodder & Stoughton, 1985).
Cowley, Robert (ed.), *What If?* (London: Pan-MacMillan, 1999).
Macdonell, A.G., *Lords and Masters* (Stroud: Fonthill, 1936, reprinted 2022).
Massie, Robert, *Nicholas and Alexandra* (London: Random House, 1967).
Spignesi, Stephen, *In the Crosshairs* (New York: Skyhorse Publishing, 2016).
Taylor, A.J.P., *The First World War* (London: Penguin, 1963).
Withington, John, *Assassins' Deeds* (London: Reaktion Books, 2020).

Magazines/Newspapers
BBC History Magazine (various).
Enter Stage Right (2008).
The Guardian (14 September 1977).
History Today (various).
The Literary Review (December 2002–January 2004).
New Statesman (June 2021).
New York Times (27 November 1963, 2 December 1963).
Time Magazine (1934).
Times Union (August 2012).

Websites
https://ultimateclassicalrock/george,harrison.
https://en'wikipedia.org/wiki/Gaelano-Bresci.
https://history.com.
https://en.wikipedia.org/wiki/Bloody-Sunday-(1905).
https://bing.com/search?+czar-nicholas.
https://en.wikipedia.org.wiki-Karl-Leibnacht.
https://en.eikipedia.org.wiki -Rosa-Luxenberg.
https://en.wikipedia.org/wiki.Cairo-Gang.
www.??history.com/this-day-in-history/syalin-banishes-trotsky.
https://bing/search-heydricj-reinhart.
hrrps://Wikipedia.org/wiki/Victor-Jara.
https://historystockexchhange.com.
https://simple.wikipedia.org/wiki/Josip-Broz-Tito.
https://thenation.com/article/archive.CIA-kennedyplot-kill-Castro.

Dear Reader,

We hope you have enjoyed this book, but why not share your views on social media? You can also follow our pages to see more about our other products: facebook.com/penandswordbooks or follow us on X @penswordbooks

You can also view our products at www.pen-and-sword.co.uk (UK and ROW) or www.penandswordbooks.com (North America).

To keep up to date with our latest releases and online catalogues, please sign up to our newsletter at: www.pen-and-sword.co.uk/newsletter

If you would like a printed catalogue with our latest books, then please email: enquiries@pen-and-sword.co.uk or telephone: 01226 734555 (UK and ROW) or email: uspen-and-sword@casematepublishers.com or telephone: (610) 853-9131 (North America).

We respect your privacy and we will only use personal information to send you information about our products.

Thank you!